The Best Of Times

Keith Jennison

On Becoming A Book Publisher

The

BEST

Of

TIMES

Marshall Jones Company
Publishers Since 1902
Manchester Center, Vermont

Library of Congress
Catalog Card Number 95-075081

I.S.B.N. 0-8338-0221-6 (hardcover)
I.S.B.N. 0-8338-0222-4 (paperback)

Printed in the United States of America

BOOKS BY KEITH JENNISON

Fiction
The Green Place
The Great International Novel Formula
From This to That

Nonfiction
Vermont Is Where You Find It
The Maine Idea
Dedication
New Hampshire
New York and the State It's In
Green Mountains and Rock Ribs
The Half-Open Road
The Boys and Their Mother
The American Indian Wars (with John Tebbel)
Remember Maine
The Humorous Mr. Lincoln
Yup... Nope and Other Vermont Dialogues
Year-Around Conditioning for Part-Time Golfers
(with Dr. William A. Pratt)
New England in the Off-Color Season
Vermonters and the State They're In

Editor
The Essential Lincoln
The Concise Encyclopedia of Sports
My Room In The World (for Catherine Phillips)

To Jack Tebbel,
the Boswell of American book publishing,
and all the other great companions

The Best Of Times

At the close of a TV program celebrating his 85th birthday, George Burns, the grand old man of vaudeville, radio, screen and TV, spoke of the hardships and disappointments of his early days in the entertainment world. He finished by turning directly to the audience and saying, "You have to fall in love with what you do for a living."

I was lucky. I fell in love with books before I learned to walk. Inevitably I fell in love with book publishing and have spent most of my life in it—a process something like dating a sequence of girls and ending up marrying one of their mothers.

In one of my not-frequent-enough times with Robert Frost I told him that his poem "Two Tramps in Mudtime" identified my feeling about book publishing far better than I could. By the time I got around to telling him exactly what the poem meant to me we knew each other well enough to argue about which one of us had the better right to be called a Vermonter.

I was brought up mostly in the family homestead in Swanton, Vermont which had been built in the late 1790's. My younger brother Peter was the fifth generation to be born in the same room of the house. I had been born in Winnipeg, Ontario because, I have always claimed, my father took my mother on a business trip when he shouldn't have. I used to take a lot of kidding from my friends about being a foreigner, but my great-aunt Jane told me not to mind because, as she put it, I was made in Vermont.

Robert's right to being a Vermonter was based on his wish to be one—instead of a New Hampshireman, for reasons known best to Robert—and Vermont enthusiastically concurred. Of course he had been born in San Francisco, about as far away from Vermont as you can get and stay on dry land, but he had taken up residence in Vermont in 1920.

The matter was settled amicably enough in 1944 during my time at Henry Holt and Company. A new collection of his poems came out and he wrote in my copy, "Keith from Robert, one Vermonter to another."

Fifteen years, three publishers and two wars later when I was helping Jack Tebbel start the Graduate Institute of Book Publishing at New York University I was invited to Robert's 85th birthday party at the Waldorf. I was late getting to the reception. My class of future book publishers lasted longer than I had planned—it usually did. Thinking about Robert's birthday I had read "Two Tramps" aloud to the class. I insisted that it was the best vocational poem ever written.

When I got to the Waldorf the happy hour was in full cry. It was a dense, distinguished group and the small anteroom was full of smoke—pipe, cigar and cigarette—but no evidence of critical fire.

I worked my way across to the corner where Robert was standing, greeted him and told him I had just read "Two Tramps" to my class at NYU.

"How did the 'work is play' line read?" he asked, paying no attention to the conversation I had just interrupted.

"Why, fine, Robert. It always does." I waited to see what was coming.

He was quiet for a few seconds. "I'm still wondering if the line should have a mark of punctuation."

Still wondering? Thirty-seven years after the poem was published?

The line that concerned him is in the last stanza of the poem:

> My object in living is to unite
> My avocation and my vocation
> As my two eyes make one in sight.
> Only when love and need are one,
> And the work is play for mortal stakes
> Is the deed ever really done
> For Heaven and the future's sakes.

I knew he was worrying that the "work is play" phrase might turn his verb "play" into a noun and the powerful, active "play for mortal stakes" be lost or misconstrued. I looked into the old, craggy face and smiled. It never occurred to me to ask what mark of punctuation he had considered.

Now that I have had a hand in the publishing of many books and written enough of my own to be accepted as an author, I'll write about my years in the world of book publishing. It is a personal story that has no plot. No rise from obscurity to fame. No rags and no riches, only memories and gratitude for having had a place in the long procession of those who had visions of what books could mean in people's lives.

I cannot remember not being able to read. Apparently I missed that miraculous moment when the letters C...A...T became the warm, purring thing in my arms.

The room I shared with my older brother Ned had built-in corner bookshelves, small standing bookcases and closets full of books mixed in with old baseball gloves, tennis racquets, shin guards, skates and golf clubs.

When the weather did not permit outdoor activity I read—with about as much selectivity as a hungry rabbit in a field of clover. The shelves were crammed with books of all kinds. *The Boy Allies at the Battle of Jutland* was pressed between *Candide* and *The Young Pitcher* by Zane Grey. The Tom Swift series was interspersed with volumes of poetry by Carl Sandburg, Rupert Brooke, Edgar Guest and Robert W. Service. I didn't care who had put this helter-skelter of books together or how they had found their way to the boys' room. They were books, so I read them.

Of all the days I spent in that world of a room, one day in particular has a clarity and content that I have thought about a lot over the years.

I sat in my brother's Morris chair reading an historical romance by Jeffrey Farnol, listening to Strauss waltzes played on a hand-cranked Victrola and glancing up from time to time at Maxfield Parrish's creation of a beautiful, naked, young boy or girl—I was never sure which but the long hair made me pretty sure it was a girl—seated on a magical swing moving through space against a luminous blue sky. I was the happiest kid in Vermont.

The weather outside was horrible and the house was full of relatives who seemed to have nothing better to do than patrol the halls and keep me under surveillance. Before the day was over they all had asked me the same questions. Why was I not reading a better book, listening to better music or looking at a better painting.

I tried to be polite and decided not to ask them what made a better book better, better music better, and a better painting better. I didn't have any idea what I might get for an answer, but was pretty sure I wouldn't like it. Later on I did ask the question of people I hoped might have some helpful answers but I never got any. Many years later I found the answer in myself.

Two of the books that I remember with great fondness were *Penrod* by Booth Tarkington and *The Tennessee Shad* by Owen Johnson. Both titles were published, singularly enough, in 1911—the year of my birth. I loved Johnson's tales of life at Lawrenceville School, but they gave me a taste for boarding school life that was not fulfilled in the austere precinct of St. Paul's in Concord, New Hampshire.

Another book that influenced me deeply was *Nonsense Novels* by Stephen Leacock, professor of political science at McGill University. I marvelled at the inspired lunacy of the humor that erupted from so distinguished a scholar. The book must have had a great deal to do with my decision to major in political science when I went to college.

After one concentrated year of study at Williams College and a semester and a half of course work at the University of Toronto's Trinity College I concluded that there was no science in things political and that the same ground covered by the learned James Bryce was dealt with much more concisely and accurately by Sir William Gilbert and Sir Arthur Sullivan.

Now that I have given my memory a license to explore any territory it chooses I can easily identify two books that guided me to the blending of my vocation and my avocation.

Mooncalf and *The Briary Bush* by Floyd Dell were both published in the middle twenties by Alfred Knopf. The bindings were imaginative and handsome, the typography was a delight and the color and texture of the paper a joy. That adult books could be beautiful artifacts gave a new dimension to the reading experience.

Many years later when I was introduced to Mr. Knopf himself, he seemed to have a sort of splendor about him—a kind of modern day Lion of Judah presence in figure and dress. The Knopf imprint stood, and stands for, excellence in editorial selection and typography. It has identified many books that have had great influence on American literary taste.

Floyd Dell's stories were compelling and the fictional characters became all the more alive to me because they were dealing with real problems in a real world. The joy I took in Parnassus, Camelot, and Sherwood Forest never diminished. All that happened was that my commitment deepened to the printed word and those who write it.

I've forgotten which summer it was I went to work as a cub reporter and gofer for the St. Albans Vermont *Daily Messenger.* My boss was Joe Fountain, who had achieved a certain fame as the only newspaper reporter present at the inauguration of Calvin Coolidge in the lamp-lit sitting room of the Coolidge homestead.

Joe advised me to spend words the way Calvin spent money— frugally. He wanted them short too.

"When you start writing for the magazines you'll get paid by the word. You'll never get paid by the syllable."

Joe did print a few short paragraphs that I wrote about meetings of various clubs and winners of baking contests at local churches. I began to write what I hoped were poems, and sent them off to small magazines. They were usually returned with a note that said that preference was always given to subscribers. It was the first of many lessons in the economics of publishing.

I was away at boarding school when the stock market collapsed in 1929. Our standard of living was lowered some but my father's business survived. Two young men, employees of a family friend who lived close to us, jumped out of windows of their office building a week after they had been throwing the football around our backyard with my brother and me.

I knew that millions of families had been wiped out—all their so-called security represented by engraved stock and bond certificates turned into junk. I was never able to equate money and security. Years later, during a long philosophical evening with Gene Fowler at the men's bar at the Waldorf, he repeated his frequently quoted opinion that money was for throwing off the ends of trains.

I didn't go that far, but I never was able to equate money with security nor indeed, to conclude that there even was such a thing as security.

After the death of my father in the winter of 1932 I came back to the Vermont homestead with my mother to straighten things out and make plans for the future. The immediate concern was financial. My father had been an entrepreneur whose income had highs and lows as dramatic, but not as predictable, as the tides in the Bay of Fundy. He had, however, managed to protect his family from most of the privations caused by the depression.

It is doubtful that what we did was what we planned to do. The family philosophy seemed always to have held that there wasn't much sense in not crossing a bridge just because you weren't sure what was on the other side. The homestead was secure, my older brother was gainfully employed, my older sister was married to a fine man who was not only employed, but worked for a solidly established publishing house that he would one day inherit from his father. My younger brother Peter still had some years of schooling ahead before he could join the work force.

My mother decided that what she needed was a long sea voyage to recover her emotional stability. She bought a round-the-world ticket on the Dollar Line, whose ships sailed weekly from New York. My own plans for the immediate future were left up to me. I could either put some of the available funds toward finishing college, or buy another Dollar Line ticket and see something of the world. I decided on the second choice.

The part-cargo, part-passenger vessels maintained a weekly schedule and our tickets were good on any of the ships. Consequently my mother and I were sometimes on the same ship and sometimes not.

It's difficult for me to draw any conclusions about what I learned from visiting places that had been only magic names as I was growing up: Shanghai, Hong Kong, Singapore, Bombay, Cairo, Rome, Paris, London...

In Shanghai, using an out-of-date press card from the St. Albans *Messenger*, I sat in on a press conference offered by Kuomintang officials on the subject of the Japanese invasion of Manchuria two years before. I was allowed a question and I asked how long the Chinese rulers thought the Japanese occupation would last.

I was answered in perfect English. The official said, "Not long, we give them a hundred years at the most."

In Bombay I talked with a young Hindu with whom I shared a taxi. He told me I must not be upset by the sight of ragged bodies of people on the sidewalk who had died of starvation during the night. We spoke of India's conflicting religions. He said there were many roads to the top of the mountain. When we parted he gave me his beautifully engraved business card. It displayed his name, his address, and in the lower corner a line that read: "Failed B.A. University of Calcutta."

In Rome I sat in the Coliseum listening for the thunder of chariots, the roaring of wild beasts and the raucous cries of geese.

The Sistine Chapel affected me so powerfully that I still regard the ceiling as the ultimate achievement of a painter's genius.

I left my ship in Genoa and took a train to Cannes. I knew all about life on the Riviera from Fitzgerald and others, but it seemed to be the wrong time of year for anything fascinating so I hired a ride up a rising road toward the Alpes Maritimes and a small town I had heard about. My road took me through hundreds of acres of roses, violets and hyacinths surrounding the city of Grasse, one of the world's great perfume centers.

Not too many kilometers beyond Grasse I found the ancient small town I had heard about. It goes by the name of St. Paul, but nobody seems to know what name the Romans gave it. Town life revolved around one of the loveliest of fountains in the village square where we came to fill our water pitchers every morning.

The room I rented was in one of the oldest parts of the settlement and the steps to my room were six-foot oblongs of heavy slate. They bore the marks of horses' hooves because, my landlady told me, the noble who lived there during the Dark Ages used to ride his horse up to his bedroom door.

Some of the old walls had crumbled, but one could still walk a good deal of the circumference of the town. Usually there was a soft wind carrying the scent of wild thyme and rosemary.

I spent the better part of a month trying to finish a novel I had been working on with more enthusiasm than judgment. One day, perhaps to seek inspiration, I walked to Vence to inspect the house D.H. Lawrence lived in for a while. I didn't find inspiration but I did find Pernod—a drink as close to absinthe as the law allowed.

Somehow I associated absinthe with great French poetry so I drank a few glasses of the greenish-yellow, cloudy liquid. I don't remember walking back to St. Paul, but the next morning at the fountain several ladies laughed solicitously as I poured water over my throbbing head.

"Mal aux cheveux," they observed. I finally concluded that their reference to the sickness of my hair was their phrase for having a hangover.

But not even St. Paul could be a "forted residence 'gainst the tooth of time"—(I wish W.S.'s lines would stop interfering with the search for my own)—and I had to get started home.

I drove to Marseilles with a friend and stayed long enough to be rowed around the Chateau d'If, that Alcatraz of the Mediterranean, so I could pay my respects to the ghost of the prisoner who became the Count of Monte Cristo.

In Paris I took a room at the Hotel St. Ives, one of the smallest of the Left Bank lodging places. From my room I could hear the hunchback ringing the great bells of Notre Dame. Through the kindness of a friend I spent one afternoon with Gertrude Stein and Alice B. Toklas in their apartment on the Ile de la Cité. I remember how warm and welcoming they were and how I felt sitting in Hemingway's chair looking at the walls crowded with portraits of my hostess by Impressionist masters. I understood everything she said about a number of things. The subject of roses did not come up.

After a fortnight of sight-seeing and visits to the Shakespeare Head bookstore I had to leave for London to be sure of catching my boat home.

I was dutifully sick on the Channel crossing but I enjoyed a conversation with a British officer returning from a two-year posting in India. The conversation was superficial to the point of exchanging information on what each of us was going to do first upon arrival in London. I admitted that I was going to start looking for the streets I wanted to walk on—Fleet, Regent, Downing, Threadneedle, Half Moon and, of course, Baker.

My short stay in London was marked by a suitable range of sunshine, rain, and fog. But I found everything I wanted most to see and it was all as I knew it would be.

The "American Farmer" took me aboard for the passage home.

I was assigned an upper berth under a porthole. The porthole came in handy as I read the manuscript of my unfinished novel and slid the pages one by one, ceremonially, into the sea. It was my first act of editing.

Soon after I had returned from my voyages I apprenticed myself to Vrest Orton, a Weston, Vermont printer/writer/editor. Vrest was cantankerous, opinionated, stubborn, and as intellectually stimulating as his former employer (and role model) H.L. Mencken. Furthermore he was a master typographer and printer.

I paid a modest fee for my room and board and the chance to learn the printer's trade. After all, working for a printer hadn't done Ben Franklin or Walt Whitman any harm. I hoped there might be some alchemy in the process.

The composing room of the newspaper I had worked for was no mystery to me, but there was no magic in the setting of lines of metal type by striking typewriter-like keys. I wanted to handle the actual type itself, experiment with letter spacing, word spacing and decide what the distance between the lines should be.

The Orton print shop was in the rear of one of the most beautiful Georgian brick houses in Vermont and contained three job presses of varying sizes. The type was kept in shallow wooden trays called—for a reason I never understood—California job cases. Each tray had almost ninety little compartments to hold the individual letters. The first thing you had to learn was where each piece of type belonged so you could put it back after the job had been run.

Vrest was an accomplished designer, but we had only one type face so his choice of style was restricted to Caslon Old Face, a beautiful type face named after the first man in England to print from moveable type. I found it exciting to handle the solid little letters and think of how they had changed the course of civilization.

He printed all sorts of things: letterheads, auction notices, garage sale flyers, Christmas cards, programs for the Weston Playhouse, broadsides of poetry we liked. Every year I remember setting type for the poem of a Brooklyn writer whose name I can't recall, but the opening couplet of his anti-war poem haunts me:

"Now in summer green and glad
Only the mind of man is mad."

Money was hard to come by. Sometimes we were paid in kind. One dairyman paid us in milk and cottage cheese, another farmer in dressed rabbits ready for stew pot. We regularly turned out posters for dances in the loft of the Parkhurst General Store and took our pay in canned goods. Selecting cans was a gamble. In the rear of the store there was a bin containing cans whose labels had been scraped off in shipping. These cans were a lot cheaper than the regularly labeled stock, but you had no way of knowing what you were going to get. We won some and lost some.

Vrest and I loved popcorn and we had it in a bowl with milk most mornings for breakfast. Vrest believed there was only one way to make popcorn. He took a round-bottomed iron kettle, melted some lard in the bottom and added a few kernels of popcorn. When the test kernels popped he poured in the rest of the kernels. He had a long and vitriolic correspondence with a New Hampshireman who claimed that popcorn popped in anything but bear grease wasn't worth eating.

Vrest was a man in rebellion against the frailties of mankind—especially as they affected him. He worked constantly and furiously at many projects—some of them mutually exclusive. He loved and respected his neighbors, but behaved as though he'd be damned if he'd let them find it out.

Our well failed that summer and we got our water next door from our neighbor's pump. One day I got back from Rutland to find Vrest, dressed in bathing trunks, scrubbing out the round granite horse trough in the center of town. He claimed to one and all that he'd rather drink after the horses of Weston than some of the people.

It turned out that he and our water-supplying neighbor had disagreed about a recent action taken by the Vermont legislature.

I learned a lot from Vrest. His standards for good typography were as high as Alfred Knopf's and Bruce Rogers'. His insistence on quality paper and precise presswork were printing and publishing precepts that stayed with me for a long time.

We parted when I decided that my road led to New York and the search for a job in book publishing, but I kept close track of him as the years passed.

A few years after I left, Vrest gave up printing and publishing and opened the Vermont Country Store. His father had been a store keeper in northern Vermont and Vrest knew exactly how to run one. He ran his store the way his father had taught him: offer good quality merchandise at a fair price. As the store became more and more successful Vrest decided to experiment with a mail order catalogue. He wrote the copy for the catalogue as if he were talking to neighbors with a responsibility for the worth of what he was selling. His son Lyman, who inherited the business, remembers carrying the first bundle of catalogues to the Weston post office. Lyman writes the same kind of copy that Vrest used to. This may be an old fashioned virtue, but in 1988 ten million of the catalogues were distributed. The success of this kind of honest writing in a merchandising field fertilized with pure hype is something to be grateful for.

The time with Vrest was also the time I was growing closer to a girl named Emily Slocum to whom, at this writing, I have been married for over 50 years.

I left Weston and Vrest with regret. Along with teaching me the basics of printing and typography he had encouraged me to try to find a way to present the best of Vermont humor in book form. I didn't find the right arrangement of text and photographs for some years after I had left Weston, but I treasured—and used—some of the caustic Vermont dialogues that I heard first from Vrest.

One of these exchanges I always associate with Vrest himself. A visitor to Vermont asked a farmer: "What do you raise around here?"

The farmer, without interrupting the rhythm of his swinging scythe, said:

"Men."

Much as I loved Vermont and Vermonters I realized that my interest in writing and printing had led me to a commitment to the world of books and if this was to be my vocation I'd have to look for a job in Boston, New York or Philadelphia. I chose New York.

When I got to Manhattan I saw evidences of the Depression in soup kitchen lines and thin, sad faces of men selling apples and pencils on street corners. I found a hotel of sorts on New York's East Side which offered units of three small bedrooms and a bathroom at a very reasonable rate. The shared bathroom soon introduced me to Arthur Dann, a student of the piano and composition at the David Mannes School, and Alex Szuwalski, a fiercely dedicated young violinist.

The hotel needed restoration, but the water ran and towels and sheets were changed before they became offensive. The small dining room offered dinners of dubious quality and were priced accordingly. But even those prices were too much for our budgets, so we worked out a deal with the management. Danny and Alex played violin and piano compositions of incredible banality during the dinner hour and I gave contract bridge lessons in the lobby. We ate in the kitchen.

Tramping around the city looking for a job in book publishing was rewarding in many ways, but no job offers resulted. I had enthusiasm and a hunger to learn, but no hireable skills.

My resume was not dishonest, but it may have been slightly misleading. The resume stated that I had been educated at Williams College and the University of Toronto. It did not state that I earned degrees from either. Neither, as in the case of the business card of my Indian friend, did it advertise that I had not. I took some comfort in thinking about Horace Greeley and George Jones who had come to the big city from Vermont apprenticeships with a lot less formal schooling than I had. Horace Greeley founded the *New*

York Tribune and George Jones became a distinguished editor of *The New York Times*.

Other Vermonters were known to book publishing. The first Henry Houghton had come from *The Burlington Free Press* to partnership in a distinguished firm. I had worked for the same newspaper. The brilliant John Farrar was a Vermonter whose family roots and mine were interwoven. John and I tried to figure out just how we were related but failed. We settled for calling each other coz and agreeing that we had common ancestors. (The phrase was John's.)

Most of the famous publishing houses granted job interviews and were friendly and generous with their time. The patrician Henry Hoyns of the House of Harper told me a great deal about the history of book publishing in America and how many publishers had started their careers as booksellers.

Mr. Hoyns was going on about the very early bookseller/ publishers and he mentioned a name that was familiar. He spoke of William Ticknor's establishment in the 1830's. The store became a rendezvous for authors and other literary people. One of these Mr. Hoyns identified as the eccentric poet John G. Saxe who, the story went, was accustomed to lying full length on a packing table in the rear of the store with his head on a pile of books, reciting poems to the apprentices.

"John Godfrey Saxe?" I asked.

"I believe so, why do you ask?"

I told him that the eccentric poet was my great-great uncle and I had been reading his delightful humorous verse since childhood.

"Maybe you have bookselling and publishing blood in you," Mr. Hoyns said as he showed me to the door of his office.

George Palmer Putnam was so welcoming that I got the impression that he was lonely. He didn't have a job for me and something in his manner suggested that he wasn't sure he had one of his own. He confessed that he hadn't seen much of Amelia Earhart since he married her in 1931.

After three or four weeks of walking, waiting, delighting in the reading room of the New York Public Library, and lowering my sights, I did get a job—and a paying one too in a strange sort of way.

I went to work for a publication called *New York in Your Pocket*.

This was a weekly magazine containing listings of movies, plays, concerts, restaurants and events of all kinds. It also carried syndicated columns and cartoons. The editor wanted a book review column in the hope of attracting advertising from the publishers. There was no salary attached to the position, but the reviewer could keep the copies of the books that publishers sent in for review and sell them to Schulte's book store for about a dollar apiece.

I accepted the appointment instantly. Now I could write to family and friends that I had become a literary critic for a New York magazine.

The editor had made it clear that he would not print a review of mine that had adverse opinions of any book that had been sent to us for review. This restriction caused an immediate problem. No one seemed to be sending us books that could cause anything but adverse opinions. I had to come up with a column of some sort every week or lose some eating money, so I took to rewriting the publisher's own descriptions of the books as they appeared on the books' jackets. I realized that I had become a member of the oldest profession, but I resolved not to practice it any longer than was absolutely necessary.

In those days you could ride the New York subways day and night for a nickel—and a lot of people did. One morning after breakfast at Nedick's—orange drink, doughnut and coffee 15 cents—I realized I had spent my last 15 cents. Danny and I were both on small allowances from our families, but he was not within reach as a banker. I walked to the magazine office and found three new books awaiting my verdict. I quickly copied off some key phrases and started for Schulte's. It was a long subway ride to Schulte's and I didn't have a nickel. I estimated a taxi ride would cost less than a dollar so I hailed a cab.

When we got to the store I asked the driver to wait and ran in with my books. The regular clerk who bought reviewer's copies was unavailable. While he was being located I could hear nothing but the ticking of the taxi meter. Finally the right man appeared, gave the books the lengthiest examination in my experience and reluctantly gave me three dollars.

The taxi meter read $2.25. I gave the driver a quarter tip and said I'd decided to walk home.

After a few months the hotel management closed the restaurant due to an almost complete lack of customers willing to eat there. This put an end to the playing-for-dinner deal that Danny and Alex had going and coincided with my exhausting all the bridge expertise that I had learned from my grandmother and my great-aunt Jane who had played whist, auction and contract all their lives—except on Sundays.

Alex decided to go to Boston where he had heard there were jobs, and Danny and I took a furnished room on East 40th Street. The room was in an old brownstone and unbelievably contained a concert grand Bechstein. The current landlady, a Mrs. Danowitz, had no idea what it was doing there and she hated it because it took up most of the room, making rentals hard to come by. It was a single room, of course, but Danny conned another mattress out of Mrs. Danowitz by promising to sleep on the piano while I slept on the daybed. An adjoining small room was just large enough to contain a full-size gas stove and a bathtub. The toilet was in the hall. The original use of the rooms was beyond speculation. So too was the method used to get the great Bechstein into the larger room. Since it could never be removed, Danny didn't worry.

No young man ever had a more delightful roommate than Arthur Dann. He was talented, humorous, interested in all kinds of music and was an innovative jazz pianist as well as a very serious classical musician. I never met anyone who didn't enjoy his playing except Mrs. Danowitz.

Danny's debut as a concert pianist had been scheduled several months in the future with the Worcester, Massachusetts Philharmonic. He had chosen to play the Saint-Saens Second Piano Concerto and asked if I would be willing to help him practice by learning to imitate what the orchestra was doing while he was playing the piano. I did the best I could which further enraged Mrs. D., who would pound on the ceiling from below with the handle of her mop. This naturally brought down pieces of plaster on her head but was clearly the fault of her crazy tenants.

She put up with us for two reasons: the first that we were paying one and a half times the single rate, and the other because after Danny's successful debut we played and sang songs from a musical comedy we started to write. She liked this music much better than the Saint-Saens concerto. We even heard her humming one of Danny's tunes one day.

The alcove or whatever it was that had the stove and the bathtub in it, contained no dishes or cooking pots or pans so we never cooked or ate anything in the room. We ate most of our meals at the nearest Automat. The food was plain but excellently prepared and the amount you could buy with a pocketful of nickels was unbelievable. I found out years later that Horn & Hardart—owners of all the Automats—bought only the best of produce and the chefs who prepared the food were highly ranked internationally.

It was a fine, companionable time. Movies were cheap, we found inexpensive seats for plays and concerts. Most of our friends didn't have any more spending money than we did, but once in a while we would make the guest list of a debutante's coming-out festivities and get a chance to mingle with the wealthy.

Finally I was offered a real job in a real publishing house. The pay was not much, but it was regular. My duties were to help pick, pack, and wrap packages in the shipping room of A.S. Barnes & Company, a hundred-year-old publisher of all kinds of text books having to do with sport. The world of text books was not exactly what I had in mind as a career, but they were books and they were good books that had a place in the schools and colleges of the country. I knew from reading Horatio Alger that where a young man started was not at the top, and besides, the man who had given me the job was the son of the owner and my brother-in-law John Lowell Pratt. Lowell was my true and supportive friend for the rest of his life.

It turned out that I enjoyed my work much more than I thought I was going to. A.S. Barnes was not a large publisher and there was no caste system. As long as I attended to my work in the shipping room I was welcome to talk to people in the other departments whenever they had time to answer questions.

Picking books from storage bins to make up shipments to schools and colleges all over the country was a real introduction to methods of book distribution. The Barnes' books covered sports from acrobatics to wrestling. I became aware of patterns of interest both in teaching and coaching. Some orders were puzzling. What would a college in Southern Florida want with ten copies of *Ice Hockey for Beginners?* I began to understand the function of sending free copies in advance to critics and opinion makers. As an auditor of periodic sales conferences I learned where the Barnes salesmen went and why.

And it all had to do with the world of sport—a world in which many of my school teachers had observed I was more at home than the realm of academia.

I had played three sports a year almost since kindergarten and semi-pro baseball summers with my brother in the as-yet-to-be organized Northern League. I had also caddied at the local country club where caddies were allowed to play after five on Thursdays.

There were valuable lessons to be learned on the playing fields. Some of the lessons were imprinted on me by coaches and others by my father who played for the patriarch of American football, Amos Alonzo Stagg.

Mr. Stagg's teams had won more games than those of any other coach in the history of football—until his record was surpassed by Alabama's Bear Bryant in 1981. Mr. Stagg placed great emphasis on character. He held that a man's personal honor was at stake in the way he played the game. It was not uncommon for coaches to lead their players in prayer before a game, but Mr. Stagg's teams did not pray for victory—they prayed to do their best. There could be honorable defeat as well as dishonorable victory.

I did not welcome the new sports creeds proclaimed by Leo Durocher: "Nice guys finish last" and Vince Lombardi: "Winning isn't everything, it's the only thing."

Sometimes I feel real sadness when I realize how many young men and women now play the games only for money and whose prestige, sense of accomplishment and fulfillment depend on the size of their incomes.

However, the status of amateur athletes did deserve, and got, a long overdue clarification. Amateur tournaments of various kinds were attracting more and more spectators. Where there were spectators there was money and most of the amateurs needed money, but couldn't accept any without losing their amateur standing. Some of us lost our virginity without even realizing it.

The summer baseball games that my brother and I played drew modest audiences. No admission was charged, but a collection was taken up. After the game the manager would come to each of us, drop a bat at our feet and bet us two dollars, or whatever the agreed upon sum was, that we couldn't jump over the bat. Strictly speaking we weren't getting paid, according to our understanding of the rules, and our virtue was intact.

But we were wrong. In 1932 both my brother and I were on the Olympic hockey squad that went to Lake Placid to prepare for the winter games. After a glorious week we were sent home. Someone had decided that we had been deflowered by our summer baseball activities. The hockey gold medal was won that year by Canada, which partially made up for my being born there instead of Vermont.

Little by little the methods of getting money into the pockets of amateur athletes became so intricate and exasperating that the establishment gave up on the whole issue, and permitted so-called "Open" meets and tournaments. For reasons best known to its members, the United States Golf Association still distinguishes between amateur and professional golfers. Even with this exception, professional athletes have risen far above their former status as paid entertainers.

One of the first things I learned at Barnes was the difference between "trade" and "text" publishing. Text books were designed primarily for use in schools and colleges. Trade books were aimed at the general reader.

Six months after I joined Barnes, my brother-in-law decided to break a hundred-year tradition and publish a trade book. It had been written by a friend of his and was called *Grand Slam, the Rise and Fall of a Bridge Wizard.*

This was the first book I was ever involved with from manuscript to bookseller. Step by step I nursed it from a typescript to printed proof sheets, then to numbered page proof, and finally to the printed cloth-bound book. I had been part of the discussions about the jacket design and illustration, I had written the jacket copy, (remembering the books I had reviewed for *New York in Your Pocket*), prepared and sent out news releases about the author.

Then I went out to take orders from wholesalers and retailers, secure in the knowledge that an audience of—no one could calculate—millions and millions of bridge players was waiting for just such a book.

My excited, confident sales pitch aroused no enthusiasm whatever. The buyers told me that the number of people who played bridge would probably define the possibilities of a book on how to play better bridge, but they thought it doubtful that all these avid, dedicated bridge players would flock to read about the adventures of a fictional bridge player by an unknown author.

I took orders for a few copies here and there with the agreement that they could be returned if unsold. The book went unnoticed by the press with the exception of a bridge magazine that panned it, and sold but a few hundred copies. No publishing lesson I learned in later years was more valuable. Market research will identify a particular area of interest, but will not tell you how many books this audience will consume.

I became a regular reader of the magazine of the book publishing industry, *Publishers Weekly*. The first time I opened it and looked at the masthead I saw, above the names of the publisher, editor and members of the staff, a quotation from Francis Bacon:

"I hold every man a debtor to his profession;
from the which as men of course do seek to
receive countenance and profit, so ought they
of duty to endeavour to themselves by way of
amends to be a help and ornament thereunto."

I found the syntax strangled, but the message was clear and by this time I was beginning to understand what made book publishing a profession as well as a business.

The months went by at Barnes and I began to hope that a more challenging and promising opportunity might appear that would get me involved in the kind of publishing I had set my heart on.

There are many maxims about getting jobs. "You have to have one to get one" and "You have to know somebody" are the familiar ones. But the people you know have to live in the right place too.

My sister and her husband lived in Darien, Connecticut and were neighbors and friends of Hastings Harcourt and his wife. Hastings was the son of Alfred Harcourt, founder of Harcourt Brace and Company which in a few years had become a prestigious publishing house. Hastings was sales manager, and at some social gathering happened to mention to my brother-in-law that he needed a New York City salesman. Two weeks later I was working for Harcourt, Brace.

When I first went into the Harcourt office at 383 Madison Avenue I was surprised by its feeling of openness. The space along the windowed walls was separated from the large central work area by a series of private offices with eight-foot-high wooden partitions. The offices had doorways but no doors and I soon found that openness and informality were qualities of the people who worked there.

At that time I didn't realize the symbolic corporate significance of the one who occupied the corner office—the one with windows on two sides. At HB the honor went to Donald Brace, Vice-President and Editor-in-Chief. This arrangement clearly stated the firm's belief that editorial quality came before anything else. Donald was a shy, reserved man greatly respected by London publishers and, in those days, many of the company's most prestigious authors were English—either by birth or adoption.

Alfred Harcourt, the CEO, was a tough, tireless man of vision, enthusiasm and a very low threshold for pettiness. He suffered fools not at all. He and Donald had gone to Columbia University together and both joined Henry Holt & Company in 1904. Fifteen years later they resigned their executive positions to found a firm of their own.

Alfred Harcourt, or A.H. as he was mostly called, was of medium height with a lined, weathered kind of outdoors face. He sometimes called himself a Dutchess County apple farmer and smoked cigarettes that he rolled from a bag of Bull Durham he kept in his shirt pocket. I felt he'd be a great man to work for. My immediate boss was his son Hastings, a complex young man who was trying to become his own man as distinguished from the one his father had planned him to be.

I hadn't thought much about salesmen one way or another until I became one. Encyclopedia salesmen used to stop by the house once in a while and my father bought an 11th edition of the *Britannica* from one of them. The set was bound in soft gray suede and was printed on the thinnest of India paper. It was such a delight to touch that sometimes I'd look up things in which I had no immediate interest just for the joy of handling the books. A Fuller Brush man called on my mother now and then and she always gave him an order. Then there were all the rural stories about traveling salesmen and farmers' daughters. But when I first hit the streets of New York carrying a sample case it seemed to me that every other man was carrying a sample case too.

My job was well defined. HB published their list of books on a more or less weekly basis, two or three new books a week. I had a list of thirty-four Manhattan and Brooklyn book dealers that I was to call on every week, show them the new books, and take orders for previously published HB books they might be out of.

I still get a feeling of excitement when I remember the books that were in continuing demand. Perhaps the title with the most lasting significance was John Maynard Keynes's *A General Theory of Employment, Interest and Money.* I know it has been a controversial book ever since it was published, but since I never really understood the book I don't understand the controversy either. But I understood and loved every word in *The Autobiography of Lincoln Steffens.* He visited the office one day and was pointed out to me as he walked down the hall. He was not physically impressive but seeing him made me understand that giants come in all sizes.

There were many other books to be proud of: recently published works as well as forthcoming books by Carl Sandburg, Virginia Woolf, T.S. Eliot, e.e. cummings. Dorothy L. Sayers, Lewis Mumford, Anne Lindbergh, John Dos Passos and others.

A delightful aspect of my new job became evident very quickly. Authors liked book salesmen. At one time or another during the first months at HB I met many of them who went out of their way to make me feel I was a welcome and not insignificant member of their publishing family. I'm sure that this was a result of A.H.'s frequently stated principle that his firm didn't publish books, it published authors.

The distinction, in case it needs clarification, was that you took on authors because you believed in their work and proposed to publish what they wrote. Some books you would like better than others, that was understood, but you would give each book its best chance. It was a partnership in the truest sense.

Of course that theory didn't always work out. Its most spectacular failure may have been in the case of Alfred Harcourt and Sinclair Lewis.

Henry Holt and Company had published several of Lewis's novels with Harcourt as editor. Lewis had unbounded faith in his own future and urged A.H. to leave Holt and start his own company to publish not only his books, but the books of other Holt authors who cared to make the move with him. A.H. had been on the best of terms with Sandburg and Frost and for a while it seemed as if both these poets would go along with the new firm. But Robert Frost, again for reasons best known to himself, decided to stay with Holt. Frost and Sandburg were not all that compatible or mutually admiring. Robert once said, "Writing poetry the way Carl does is like playing tennis without a net."

The new firm started with the novel that, so to speak, made Lewis famous. *Main Street* was a tremendous bestseller in 1920 and was followed by *Babbitt* in 1922. In 1926 *Arrowsmith* was awarded the Pulitzer Prize but Lewis turned it down. *Elmer Gantry* shocked and captivated the American reading public in 1927 and in 1930 Lewis won the Nobel Prize for Literature—the first American to be so honored.

This sounds like a wonderfully rewarding publishing relationship. It was, for Lewis. For Alfred Harcourt it had some of the aspects of a nightmare. Lewis used Alfred as editor, messenger boy and healer of ego wounds who must be available at bedside or barside at any hour of the day or night. As his fame grew so did his demands.

The end came as a result of Lewis's constant demands that A.H. produce a matched set of his novels. Alfred told me of countless phone calls insisting on the immediate production of the set with details about how the books should be bound and what kind of paper must be used.

"The last call,"Alfred said,"was from Red in Stockholm before the Nobel ceremonies. He attacked me in a fury because the set was not ready for the occasion. I listened to him for a while and when he stopped to catch his breath I told him the set had been in preparation for months, but we hadn't started the composition until the Nobel prize had been announced. That really sent him off in a rage of personal abuse."

A.H. paused and rolled a Bull Durham. "I held my hand over the phone and asked my secretary to bring me the Lewis contract. When I got it in my hand I put the phone down and began to rip the contract into pieces. Red heard something and asked what the noise was. I told him it was me tearing up his contract. Then I hung up." He turned to me with a slow smile and said,"We all have our limits."

I had to pass his office at the end of the day when I took my orders to the order desk. Sometimes he would wave me in and ask how things were going.

Almost without exception the booksellers were warm and welcoming. My job was really quite simple. I showed them the new books, told them what I had learned about the author, and tried to make sure they bought the right number of copies. They had no reason, yet, to know whether my advice on what they might need of any particular title was worth taking or not. After all, we had a midtown shipping room and if they needed extra copies it was simple to supply them. I really learned my job, not from the Harcourt Brace editors, but from the booksellers. It was evident that if I was to be calling on them every week I had to behave so they wouldn't vanish in the stockroom when they saw me at the door. Many booksellers became friends as the weeks and months went by.

The job got more interesting all the time. When T.S. Eliot's *Murder in the Cathedral* opened on Broadway I asked my sales manager if he would give me a commission to sell our hardbound edition of the play in the lobby of the theater. He agreed, so I scavenged a card table from somewhere and set myself up for business. I didn't sell a great many books, but I saw the play thirty-seven times and never really got tired of it. I learned that actors give slightly different performances every time they play in the parts. I loved the slimy rationalizations of the murderous knights—especially the way in which the fourth knight proved to himself, if nobody else, that the great Archbishop had really committed suicide.

Another fascinating part of the experience was listening to the between-acts conversations of the audience as well as opinions after the play ended. I heard many of the same conclusions—but never expressed in the same way.

Before too long I was accepted by what was known officially as The Brotherhood of American Book Travelers. It could be a fellowship because we were not really competitive. No customer refused to buy the new book of poems by T.S. Eliot from me because he or she had just bought the new book of poems by Robert Frost from my friend who sold the city for Henry Holt.

We developed favorite restaurants and taverns where we counted on being amused by news, rumors and gossip about what was going on in our world of books and authors. Once a year we met officially for our festive Field Day, about which the less said the better.

We also sent each other advance copies of books that we thought were going to be bestsellers. Randy Williams, a classmate of mine at St. Paul's who had left the school's English faculty to become a book salesman for the Macmillan Company, sent me a book with an uninspiring title about the Civil War. I read it in a day and a night. For years I claimed that I sold more copies of *Gone With The Wind* in advance of publication than Randy did.

Some booksellers were more hospitable than others. Jack Karpf's Bryant Bookshop was a haven and a message center for quite a few of us. Jack had a small living room between his store and his bedroom which contained a very good record player and a wonderful library of recordings. On rainy days it was rare to call on Jack and not find one or more of your fellow salesmen listening to music in the back room.

Another bookstore in the posh section of upper Madison Avenue took a different view of me. I called there one day, met two of my old friends and exchanged joyful greetings while Miss Norton, the manager of the store observed the proceedings with cold dissatisfaction. When I finally reached her desk she told me not to bother to sit down or come back.

I looked into A.H.'s office as I passed it on my way to the order desk later that day. He was on the phone and when he saw me motioned me in. I remember the last part of his conversation very well.

"Miss Norton, if you want to do business with Harcourt Brace and Company you will do business with Mr. Jennison. As far as you're concerned Mr. Jennison is Harcourt Brace and Company."

He hung up, turned to me, asked what had happened, told me in no uncertain terms that my behavior was unacceptable and was not to be repeated. This was the first of many management lessons for which I am eternally grateful to Alfred Harcourt.

Being a city salesman in New York was far from being an unhealthy job. The sample case you carried weighed about twenty or twenty-five pounds and didn't get any lighter as the day passed. You climbed a lot of stairs, got on and off a lot of buses and walked the soles off your shoes. But the city was easier and less frantic then, and riding down Fifth Avenue in the sunshine on the open top of a bus was hardly a disagreeable experience.

In 1936 I felt secure and happy enough in my job to ask Emily Slocum to marry me. We were married in February 1937. Why we got married in February is beyond understanding. For a little over a year we lived in Manhattan and then we moved to Elmhurst, Long Island. This sounds a great deal more bucolic than it was. Elmhurst was, in fact, a suburb of Jackson Heights and there were few elms to be seen. I commuted to work on the 8th Avenue subway.

As I became more knowledgeable about individual bookseller's needs and the possible sales appeal of the titles I was selling, I was able to be more effective. Our discount schedule made it more profitable for the bookseller to buy in quantity if he sold all he ordered.

The first success I had loading New York booksellers with advance copies of a particular book came as a result of my friendship with one of New York's most distinguished personal booksellers, the proprietor of the Holiday Book Shop. Ted Holiday was a specialist in modern English authors. Whenever I started out with a new book by an author well known in Britain but perhaps not yet accepted by the American reading public I called on Ted Holiday first. He always gave me knowledge in depth about the author's previous books, critical reception, sales, and many more valuable insights.

When I showed him an advance copy of *The Years,* by Virginia

Woolf, he told me that it was not going to be hailed as her best book, but that it was going to be a great bestseller in the United States.

I knew of the critically acclaimed books she had published, had read parts of some of them in an admiring but not enthralled way, and was fascinated by Ted's forecast.

He explained that her international reputation had prepared the American market for a new book of hers that was stronger in story and characterization. This was the book that would capture a huge audience. He suggested that I would be doing my booksellers a favor by persuading them to buy in quantity.

I acted on his advice and began to sell the book almost as if it was the last book that would ever be published. The sales manager warned me that we would be asked to take most of them back, but the editors were delighted.

Upon publication *The Years* was given glowing, exciting reviews. *The New York Times Book Review* gave it the front page, so did the *Herald Tribune* and the *Saturday Review*. *Time* put an unflattering picture of the author on its cover. The first printing sold out in a matter of days.

A chance soon came along to climb out on another limb. The sales conference presented, in a sort of routine way, a little book of poems called *Old Possum's Book of Practical Cats.* We had imported 750 copies of this impressive item. Of course the poems were written by T.S. Eliot, but in those days the name didn't carry all that much sales weight.

But who could fail to be enchanted by the doings of cats named Mungojerrie and Rumpleteazer, Jennyanydots and Macavity the Mystery cat? I began to think of a nation of cat lovers. But, remembering the nation of bridge players, how many of them were book lovers too? My instinct directed me to The Channel Bookshop at the corner of 48th Street and Park Avenue. This charming establishment was run by two delightful, middle-aged ladies who were never called by their first names. I showed a copy of the book to Miss Fleming and Miss Anderson. Soon we were reading the poems aloud to each other.

The Channel Bookshop had loyal customers all over the country who trusted the partners to pick books for them and send them right along. We discussed the number of copies the store should order. The three of us decided that HB had made a grave error in making so few copies of this irresistible book available to the American reading public. Clearly the supply would be gone almost overnight.

Miss Fleming asked how many of the 750 copies she could order. I made a rough estimate of the number of advance copies we would need for critics, library service centers, various depositories, copies for all our salesmen and intimate friends of editors, presents to some of our authors who adored T.S. Eliot, cats, or both and added up the numbers.

I looked up at Miss Fleming, "I think we can let you have four hundred copies."

She wrote out the order and thanked me. Then I had to go back to the office and file the order. Soon after I had returned to my desk my phone rang and the order clerk asked me whether the Channel Bookshop order was for four, or 40 copies of Old Possum.

"It's for four hundred," I said.

"Oh."

In a few minutes A.H. called me. "I've just ordered an American printing of the Eliot," he said. "Do you think the Channel ladies will accept partial shipments?"

I said I was sure they would.

At this writing the musical extravaganza CATS, inspired by this collection of poems, is breaking all kinds of records.

I wasn't this right much of the time. Many, many times my enthusiasm for a particular book was misplaced, but even then, a bookseller could be relieved of overstock by one means or another. When I had to face up to my mistakes I comforted myself by thinking about Ty Cobb. He had the highest lifetime batting average of anyone who had ever played baseball. His average was .367. What made this comforting was the thought that he went to bat to use all his talent, training and experience to get a hit— and was right not much more than once out of every three times.

Of course this was comforting only as it applied to baseball. You had to do a lot better than this in being right about the books you decided to publish. Over the years the trade book publishers lost money on almost one out of every three books they published. The difference was made up by income from the publishers' share of movie and reprint rights on the successful books. These were problems I didn't have to deal with as a city salesman, but I did understand that they existed.

The big retail book season was, of course, between Thanksgiving and Christmas. This was the time that retail booksellers tried hard to keep the books in stock that were selling. Lots of times this meant that I became a delivery boy as well as a salesman. It was also a time when some customers drove bookstore clerks to distraction.

Nick Wreden, the manager of Scribner's Fifth Avenue store, told me about a scene that took place in the children's section of his store one holiday afternoon.

"One of the last members of our carriage trade," Nick said, "pulled up in front of the store in an ancient Rolls Royce. The chauffeur helped an equally ancient lady to our front door. She was dressed in formal black, with a jeweled black satin choker around her neck and carried an ebony stick with a silver handle. She walked slowly to the head of a counter and announced she wished to look at some children's books."

Nick described how the clerks galvanized, cleared a space in front of the old lady and began to show books to her one by one.

"She bent down," Nick went on, "adjusted her lorgnette and studied each offering. Then she would straighten up and say, 'Revolting, detestable, abhorrent' or longer expressions of her distaste. One by one the clerks went to other more eager customers until the least experienced clerk was left with the dowager."

You could tell Nick loved what came next by the look on his face. "The poor young man looked around for something to show that the lady hadn't already seen. Behind a row of books on the bottom shelf he found a dusty copy of one of the *Blue Ribbon Pop Up* books. [These were editions that had three-dimensional cardboard illustrations that sprang up from the spine of the book when it was opened.] The clerk clapped the dust off the volume behind his back, put it down in front of the lady and opened it. The dramatic scene of Washington crossing the Delaware popped up in full color. As the lady bent down, lorgnette in place, to inspect this offering, a cockroach climbed out of the interior workings and crawled across the page."

When Nick got to this point in the story he could hardly contain himself.

"The dowager bent down over the book, then staggered back, dropped her lorgnette and screeched, 'Intolerable, insufferable.'

"The young clerk, running out of poise and restraint, agreed. 'Lady, it sure is. That little son-of-a bitch is supposed to be carrying the American flag.'"

Many booksellers ran lending libraries to increase the store's income. Customers liked both the convenience and the economy of being able to rent new bestsellers instead of buying them. The lending libraries helped me too. I could examine the titles of other publishers, find out how well they were renting and inquire from the bookseller some of the reasons that the books were being well received or found to be disappointing. This was a sort of rudimentary market research, but it was helpful.

One aspect of hearing people make comments on books they had rented and read bothered me a good deal. A new novel or work of non-fiction would come out with heavy advertising, promotion and 21-gun salutes from the critics. All too frequently I overheard a customer return the book with the guilty comment that he guessed he "just wasn't up to it," then select a book from the mystery shelf and slink from the store as if going into seclusion to practice some shameful act of self-indulgence.

This depressing scene fired up the same resentment I had felt years before when I was put under pressure to read "better" books. I acknowledged that some books were better than others, but I was uncomfortable in not being able to define why, and in what ways.

The more I thought about it the more I became convinced that if I had finished college and taken all the literature courses that the critics had obviously taken I would know the answer.

One day I talked to Alfred Harcourt about my growing inferiority complex and said that I was going to register for evening courses at Columbia and finish my Bachelor's degree. A.H., a Columbia man himself, advised me not to. "You won't get an instructor that will interest you in the extension courses, and anyway, if you stay in the book publishing business you'll learn all you want to by yourself."

This opinion was borne out shortly. Most of the Harcourt titles were easily accessible, but we had taken on the U.S. distribution of The International Library of Psychology, Philosophy and Scientific Method.

One of the titles in the International Library was *The Meaning of Meaning* by C.K. Ogden and I.A. Richards. This title caused much comment, not all favorable. Later on we printed a guide to the book called *The Meaning of the Meaning of Meaning.* This didn't seem to help much as far as sales went.

However getting acquainted with the International Library turned out to have rewarding results. C.K. Ogden of Cambridge's Magdalene College was the General Editor so I figured that studying the books he chose would be like taking courses at Cambridge.

The first title I chose seemed aimed directly at my most immediate interest: I.A. Richards' *Principles of Literary Criticism.*

I tackled many of the books in the Library with varying results, but I was introduced to some of the finest minds of the century: Wittgenstein, Jung, Adler, Piaget, Malinowski, Bentham, Peirce and Hulme.

Of course the insights I acquired were shallow and I could not make value judgements on most of the theories I read about. However, I could listen to a discussion of them with some understanding and later on when I worked to develop an aesthetic rationale of my own I knew where to go for my tutoring.

The great times I had with Carl Sandburg started when he came to New York to do a round of readings of his poetry as a promotion to celebrate the publication of his seventh book of poetry, *The People, Yes.*

Alfred Harcourt had published Carl's *Chicago Poems* in 1916 and it well may have been one of the first books of poetry I read. I still think of Chicago as "City of the Big Shoulders," and I always associated the famous cat-footed fog with Lake Michigan until Carl told me he had written the poem in San Francisco.

The People, Yes is a book of stories, yarns and sayings of the American people along with some songs, prayers and psalms. Written in all of Carl's voices, intonations and rhythms, it is a book you can open anywhere and find questions great and small and answers great and small in the words and phrasings that the people of the country he loved had given him for the saying.

Whether the contents form one poem or a collection of many poems doesn't matter any more than how you define Walt Whitman's *Leaves of Grass.*

Carl's lecture, or recital, tour called for appearances in Manhattan, Brooklyn, the Bronx and Long Island. I sold the sales manager, with no opposition, my plan to carry books to all the performances and have them ready for people who wanted to buy autographed copies. I carried the books in twin suitcases which seemed to weigh a couple of hundred pounds, but I couldn't complain because at the same time I was paying Sig Klein's gym for supervised weight lifting routines.

All of Carl's performances had a quality of spontaneity and

delight that warmed and relaxed audiences as soon as he began to speak. His blunt farmer's face with a white fall of hair across the forehead would glow with delight, anticipating what he and his audience were going to do together.

He would start by reading some of his poems: some humorous, some tinged with melancholy and the sad acceptance of things as they are, and others ringing with conviction that people of good will would eventually prevail.

When he picked up his guitar a murmur of approval always ran through the crowd. He told me he never decided in advance what songs he would sing before he stood in front of a particular audience. As the editor of *The American Songbag* he had enough songs to last a week or more. Sometimes he would sing mostly trail songs from the push westward, other times songs from the days of the clipper ships and the whalers. And always he sang some of the New England and Appalachian versions of ancient ballads from the British Isles.

His voice was deep and thick-textured but always under control. He could whisper you a lullaby, pierce you with bitter and lonely songs of the dispossessed, or sound a warning you could hear halfway across the State of Kansas.

After the greetings, handshakings and autographing, we would pack up the guitar, what books we had left and head for a beer at the nearest tavern.

And there we talked about everything: baseball, newspapers, robber barons, poetry—he loved Emily Dickinson— Chicago gang wars, Norman Thomas, the Dust Bowl and, without fail, Abraham Lincoln. Carl had published the first two volumes of his great Lincoln biography and was well along toward finishing the work that would run to four more volumes.

It was hard to get him to talk about himself and the years he had spent in so many different jobs that I couldn't keep track of them. But in 1952 the only volume of autobiography he wrote was published. Under the entry "Sandburg, Carl, occupations," I found the following list: (page numbers omitted) barbershop porter, boathouse helper, bottlewasher, college student, drugstore chore boy, firehouse call man, handbill distributor, hobo, icehouse worker, mail-order businessman, milkman, newsboy, office boy, painter's apprentice, potter's helper, racetrack boy, soldier, stage helper supe, tinsmith's helper, water boy. When I saw the list for the first time I thought of asking Carl why writing poetry was not listed as an occupation but decided not to.

Just as soon as I got my work week, which included Saturday mornings, well organized and comfortably arranged I was given a raise and additional territory. There were two great things about the new schedule: I was to cover booksellers in major New England cities and I was going to do it by train.

Traveling on trains had been a favorite adventure of my childhood. My mother's family lived outside Chicago and to go there for a visit meant a trip on either the "20th Century Limited" or the "Broadway Limited." The railroad stations themselves were palaces of activity and the search down the platform to find which of the sleepers was ours was exciting beyond description.

On my first business train trip I took the "Owl" to Boston. It left New York at midnight but you could board it much earlier and get a good night's sleep before your arrival in the first home of American publishing.

For a long time I lay awake in my berth thinking about the beginnings of the Bay Colony, of the founding of a college in 1636 named after John Harvard, and of the conviction that the colony could not grow and prosper without a printing press. I had first become interested in this famous printing press because it has been in Montpelier, Vermont for more than a hundred years and, I was told, would still do a pretty fair job of printing if it had to. The press came to the colonies mostly through the efforts of the Reverend José Glover who went to England with some money and raised enough more there to buy a printing press. He also found a man to run it—a locksmith named Stephen Daye who didn't know much about printing but who had a son who did.

The ship carrying the press landed in 1638 but tragically the Reverend Mr. Glover had died during the passage. The widow Glover assumed his responsibilities in the project and saw to it that the press was installed in the basement of the home of Henry Dunster. Two years later Mr. Dunster became the first president of Harvard and the widow Glover became his wife. The same year saw the production of the first book to be published in the Thirteen Colonies. The volume is known as *The Bay Psalm Book* and I can remember the thrill of looking at one of the few remaining copies.

The next morning at the Parker House I was joined at breakfast by Jack Mullen of the Viking Press. Somehow Jack had learned that this was my first trip to see the Boston accounts. With the utmost friendliness he told me exactly how the accounts should be sold— and in what order. He then suggested firmly that I join him and some other salesmen at cocktails and tell them what kind of day I had. Jack was not quite the revered figure he became in later years, but I got the message that I was joining a group of professionals who were proud of their occupation and wanted to be sure that the new people measured up to their standards.

I don't know whether or not I made all the mistakes a salesman could make in a new territory that day, but I'm sure I made most of them.

The actual sales ritual went like this. You handed the buyer your new fall or spring catalog, opened one for yourself, and showed him a sample copy of the book on page one. These dummy copies were pages from the book bound in the same cloth as the complete book, and covered by a proof of the book's jacket.

In New York City I had always sold from finished books so the buyer always knew exactly what he was taking into the store. The typography of a book mattered, the paper mattered and so did the binding and the jacket.

As the buyer glanced quickly at these essentials you described briefly the setting of the book, something about the characters and plot and the sales record of the author—provided it was a good record. If the author's most recent book had bombed, you mentioned what great reviews it had had, if indeed it had. If the reviews were bad or non-existent you just mentioned that the reviews were mixed. What this usually meant was that the book got one or two so-so reviews and lots of bad ones. Then you spoke of your firm's belief in this author and his future.

If it was a first novel, or a first book of non-fiction, you went through the same routine but reflected the confidence everyone had in the book and showed advance quotes from well known personages—if you had any.

Then the buyer would state the number of copies wanted and the salesman could reply. On my first trip I at least had sense enough to reply nothing but "thank you" and go on to the next book.

But we always fought for representation, that is, to get one or two copies of every book in all the bookstores. In those days, I figured we were doing business with about a thousand bookstores so we tried to "open" a book of fiction, non-fiction or poetry in a thousand places around the country. Then if the reviews came and our advertising and promotion worked, the basis for a growing readership and consequent re-orders could be established. We salesmen had a very simple duty—to do everything we could to make sure each book on our list got its best chance.

On some of my future trips to Boston I was to go to a few openings of plays before they opened in New York. I was always sad when I read that one had failed its first test and was to be seen no more. We could take a poet's work and open it in a thousand places where it had a chance to reach its audience and time to do it.

At the end of my first day in Boston I reported to Jack Mullen as requested. He listened to my account of the calls I had made and the people I had met, nodded approvingly several times, paid for our drinks—one apiece—announced that he was going to his room to write up his orders and suggested that I go write up mine.

That was the first of many, many fine days in the New England territory which included—for me—Springfield, Hartford, Waterbury and New Haven, as well as Boston.

My last date on my first trip was with Mercy Boyd's Bookshop in Waterbury, Connecticut. If this had been my first date I would have been much more effective with all my succeeding calls.

When I arrived at the store I was shown to a neat desk in the back of the store where a slight, attractive older woman was seated. She nodded to me and pointed to the chair drawn up to the desk beside her. Then she picked up a graceful, black ear trumpet, brought it to her ear and smiled. She was ready for me to begin.

I handed her a catalog, placed the dummy of the first book in front of her and began my sales talk. It seemed to me I was just getting started on my helpful analysis of the book and its possibilities when Miss Boyd, with another smile, put the ear trumpet back on her desk and looked at me expectantly. Clearly she had heard all she wanted to hear about the first book and wanted me to move on.

Over the next few years I developed great affection for Mercy Boyd's bookstore and the young women who worked there. On my last trip there, when gasoline was rationed, Mercy Boyd told me a story about her mother that is still one of my favorite illustrations of the New England character.

Miss Boyd's mother lived in a neighboring town in a lovely little stone house. She was an ardent rose gardener. When her milkman put his truck away for the duration of the war and went back to his horse-drawn wagon, he kept his usual precise early morning deliveries. Every morning at six-fifteen he would pull up on her immaculate, crushed stone driveway and deliver a quart of milk to the kitchen door. While he was so engaged, the horse would leave a deposit on the driveway. Every morning without fail.

Mercy's mother put up with this as long as she could. She collected enough fertilizer for acres of rose gardens. Finally, one morning in a cold fury she called the chairman of the Board of Selectmen of her town and vented her opinion in detail. Then she finally ran out of breath there was silence until the selectman said, "Well, Mrs. Boyd, I wish I was that regular."

I can still see the daring look of pleasure on Mercy's face when she told me this story.

There was much to learn about how the book business worked at the distribution level, and some of what I learned never failed to confuse me. Most publishers' advertising in newspapers and magazines concluded with the phrase, "Available at your bookseller or from the publisher." The booksellers weren't too happy about this and frequently sent me away with the request to remind my boss that no other manufacturer of anything was willing to service orders direct from consumers. When I spoke about this at the office I got, at best, an evasive answer. What it boiled down to was that this was the way it had always been. That the first American publishers had been booksellers and we hadn't quite decided to give up the practice of selling our own books to readers who wanted to buy direct.

Then there was something inexplicable, to me anyway, about the way the wholesaling function was organized. There were many book wholesalers in the East. They got fewer as you went West. Most libraries bought their books from wholesalers—on a bid basis. Many booksellers bought their stock from wholesalers too. The discount was lower, but it saved a lot of bookkeeping to have only one supplier. Publishers gave wholesalers a higher discount than retailers to perform their necessary function.

I began to get confused on my first trip to Boston when I called on a library wholesaler, or jobber, one of whose accounts was the Seattle Public Library. When I remarked that the shipping costs must be high, I was told that nobody made any money on the deal but the common carrier. But that was the way things were done.

Another thing that boggled my mind was that the jobbers had salesmen who called on retail bookstores. We gave them a preferential discount for providing this service to our books. Frequently, while I was talking with the buyer of a bookstore, a salesman from a jobber would be waiting to see the same buyer. The buyer would admit that he didn't really need both of us, but that was the way things were done.

Whenever people in book publishing—at any level—got together the subject of what made books sell always seemed to come up. And what it always came down to was "word of mouth." Reviews could take a book's sales only so far. After that it took a body of readers who spoke of that particular reading experience with excited appreciation. Advertising would sell a book that was already selling, but it would not sell a book that was not selling.

The word-of-mouth theory was tested one week by Hastings Harcourt. There was a Doubleday retail bookstore in Lord and Taylor's Fifth Avenue store. He advised the manager that on a certain day a new selling technique would be tested in the department store and asked the manager to see what happened to the sales rate of the current HB bestseller as a result.

Hastings hired a half-dozen men and women of reputable appearance to ride up and down in the elevators all day talking about what a great time they had had reading *The Perception of*

Paradise or whatever the book was called. After a week of this experiment not a single sale in the nearest bookstores could be traced to the elevator dialogues.

Another research project involved renting a meeting hall that would hold about 300 and giving the participants thin rubber bulbs to hold in their hands. These bulbs were filled with fluid and somehow connected by rubber tubing to a kind of literary seismograph that would detect the intensity and duration of emotional shock waves.

The theory was that when a manuscript was read aloud to the group the physical results of the reading would then be charted so the editor and publisher could tell when interest was at a high point, low point, or no point at all. The process was offered to publishers to assist them in making a decision as to whether or not to publish, and to authors to assist them in re-writing. I never heard of any firm or author using this service.

Almost all publishers published a spring list of books and a fall list. This resulted in their representatives taking their selling trips at approximately the same time. Why booksellers put up with these invasions of groups of publisher's reps all arriving in town together is a mystery. But they did. And they did it with grace and a seeming lack of resentment. Of course we were entertaining—if not intellectually at least gastronomically. We took them to lunch and to dinner. We invited them to poker games at night, or the movies, or the theatre if such was available. And of course there was a good deal of sociable drinking to be done.

The greatest friend to all book salesmen who covered New England may well have been Israel Witkower, whose wonderful big store was in Hartford. During the few days when the invasion was at its height and there were seven to ten of us in town there would be a daily gathering at Witkower's. Promptly at five o'clock the counters would be covered and Israel would bring out a bottle or two and we all—except the golfers who were bound for the golf course with Ralph Ong, the buyer for the Hartford branch of the giant book wholesaler, the American News Company—would knock down a few drinks while deciding where to have dinner. More often than not we were joined by the buyers from Brentano's and the G. Fox department store. When the dinner plans were agreed upon we would go back to our hotels, write up the day's orders—that was obligatory—and get ready for dinner. We liked our jobs, we liked each other and we had good times.

Years later, after the war, I came down with a bout of hepatitis and was bedded down at home. Israel Witkower found out about my illness and for two weeks I got a small package from the store—every day. Sometimes it would contain a box of paper clips, a package of small note pads, pencils, pens, erasers. No get well cards, no words of sympathy—just little packages that said all there was to say.

Just as life on the road was becoming more enjoyable so was life in the office. I began spending more time with the HB editors both in and out of the office. They were an exciting group: Cap Peirce and Sam Sloan were to form their own publishing firm, Chester Kerr would one day enter on a distinguished career at the Yale University Press, Bob Giroux went on to become a partner in Farrar, Straus and Giroux, and perhaps the man I was closest to of all—Stanley Young. There were others, of course, and I remember them all—none more clearly than Frank Morley, who introduced me to the little bar at the Ritz and taught me the virtues of unblended scotch whiskey.

But the member of the staff I saw most of, almost from the beginning, was Helen Taylor. Helen was advertising manager when I got to HB and consequently worked closely with the sales and promotion departments. Helen was an accomplished pianist who never talked about it, an honor graduate of Wells College and, due to cruel circumstances, the sole support of her mother and grandmother.

She was a tall, rangy young woman with a tough, merry face. Helen and her colleague Doris Schneider let me try my hand at writing jacket copy and promotion releases. When my corrected submissions began to get good enough they used some of them. The copy was a lot better than I had written for *New York in Your Pocket* and *Rise and Fall of a Bridge Wizard*.

Spending time with the HB editors gave me an insight into the process by which books were chosen for publication. In the first place, all submissions were read carefully and as quickly as possible. These "over the transom" manuscripts were all given serious consideration—contrary to the widely held assumption that one had to have a name or a good agent to get a fair reading. It was true that rarely was an unsolicited manuscript taken for publication, but there were exceptions. Later on in my publishing life I was credited with having "discovered" one or two successful authors. The truth of the matter is that I had gotten to the office early enough to examine what had been left on our doorstep before any other editor got around to it.

Literary agents were tremendously important in the acquisition of manuscripts. A firm's editorial, sales, and promotion reputation influenced submissions from agents. The first thing an editor did when he had read a manuscript that he felt strongly the firm should publish was to have it read by his colleagues—or at least a couple of them. The editorial board would consider all the reports and ask for more readings if Alfred Harcourt or Donald Brace needed the evidence of their own readings.

This was not publishing by committee even though it may sound that way. Members of the editorial board all had different backgrounds, different tastes, different areas of expertise, in some cases opposing political theories as well as economic and social codes. But they had one thing in common and that was a commitment to quality. No matter the subject of a work of non-fiction or the theme of a novel: if there was agreement on a manuscript's quality it might well be published against the taste of some members of the board. The two partners had veto power, but I never heard that it was used on any grounds but quality.

In rejecting a manuscript A.H. frequently closed the letter with the sentence, "You must understand that this is only our judgment, but it is the only one we have and we must be guided by it. Another publisher may well feel differently." He sought editorial advice widely and listened when it was offered. Then he went ahead and acted according to the value judgment he had arrived at.

In 1938 HB published a book that took me deeper in a most exciting way into the fields of linguistics and semantics. The book was *The Tyranny of Words* by Stuart Chase. In the very beginning he asked himself the question, "Is it possible to explain words with words?" Chase's book was much easier to read than *The Meaning of Meaning*—and it sold a lot more copies too. It marked the first time I wrote a fan letter to a New York newspaper. Book critic Ralph Thompson of *The New York Times* wrote an admiring review of the book in which he used phrases like, "...displays a sort of wholesome heresy and disrespect for absolutes that will mark the emergence of the New Sanity—when and if it ever does emerge."

That's the kind of review I liked to think about on a hot afternoon in the subway delayed under the East River on the way back from selling accounts in Brooklyn.

Another book that I still treasure was published in 1938. *The Collected Poems of e.e. cummings* was hard to sell in any quantity in spite of my personal enthusiasm for his poems. I understood that he had a limited readership.

In order to promote a wider readership we decided to issue a recording of e.e. cummings reading selections from the book. I think Cap Peirce was cummings' editor at HB Of course the word editor didn't mean much when it came to as rare an individual poet as cummings. At some point I had mentioned to Cap that I was a great admirer of cummings' work, so when it came time to take him to the studio to make the recording Cap asked me to handle it.

Completely natural and low-keyed, e.e. cummings was one of the most engaging men I had ever met. Survivor of a World War I prison camp, his strong, sensitive face and clear blue eyes gave you the impression of a man whose basic purity had never been corrupted.

Almost always when I think of cummings I remember the lines Noel Coward wrote about his friend William Bolitho: "The mind of a poet, as I see it, is a mind that has survived the squalor of small humiliations and the melancholy of great disillusions, and remains unerring in its perception of beauty in the human heart."

Some poets don't read their poems very well, but e.e. cummings read his wonderfully well and the quality of the original recording was excellent. When we were finished at the studio cummings asked me to come home with him to his apartment on Patchin Place—the most charming cul-de-sac in the city. There I met his wife, the former model Marion Morehouse. She was a lovely woman with the same calm grace as her husband.

We had tea and I looked at some of the photographs Marion had taken and some of the watercolors cummings had painted. He said he had thought of himself as a painter before he decided that poetry was the main current of his creativity.

He readily admitted that visually many of his poems were difficult to read and abided by no traditional form of poetry that he was aware of. He explained that what he was doing was taking all the typographics and punctuation marks of our language and painting with them. In some cases this technique was perplexing, but when read aloud the poems were direct and extraordinarily moving.

I told him that sometimes, in a small group of our closest friends, I read some of his poems aloud and when they looked at the printed text they sometimes, at first glance, claimed that they couldn't be the ones they had just heard.

Cummings and Marion came to our apartment for dinner a few times—it was a long subway ride to Elmhurst and Jackson Heights and we were touched and complimented that they felt like making the trip. I dropped in to see them in Patchin Place and we became close but not intimate friends. I feel sad when I think of how many times this happened over the years. There were too many authors I was involved with in one way or another to permit the slow growth of lasting relationships. But one thing happened with e.e. cummings that was very special.

One night, with one of my oldest friends and his wife, I read some of his love poems aloud. I still feel that they are among the best ever written. "Somewhere I Have Never Travelled" I was asked to read twice and my friend and his wife seemed particularly moved by it.

A few months later they told us they were going to have a baby.

"We decided that night after you read the cummings "Somewhere I Have Never Travelled."

In due course a lovely, blond, blue-eyed daughter was born and about five years later I sent cummings a picture of her and told him about the reading of his poems. He sent the little girl a charming note and one of the elephant sketches that he sometimes used as a signature.

Some years later when I was a partner in a new publishing house I used some of my clout to re-issue a book of his prose that had not been available for quite a while. His was a name I wanted to see on the list of authors we published.

There were many self-appointed censors around during those years, men and women who dedicated themselves to the task of keeping "obscenity" out of books. No one seemed to be quite sure what obscenity was, but it clearly had to do with scenes of sexual conduct in which various parts of the anatomy were referred to by name. Some of our worthiest citizens were still reeling from the shock of seeing James Joyce's *Ulysses* on sale in bookstores. Poor Lady Chatterley had no legal home in England or in the United States even though D.H. Lawrence's explicit language was intended "to burn out the oldest shames in the deepest places," as the game-keeper put it.

The general idea was promoted that reading certain books would create unhealthy appetites in people which would turn them into sexual gluttons.

Balzac may well have established this concept. About a hundred and fifty years ago he wrote some pretty lewd, for that time, short stories which were put into a volume called *Droll Stories*. He wrote an introduction for the collection saying that he wrote the stories for his own amusement and to increase the population of France. He amused a lot of people besides himself, but nothing is known about the book's effect on the French birth rate.

The Harcourt stand on this issue had been established in 1927 when Lewis's *Elmer Gantry* was banned in Boston. The Old Corner Bookstore returned a number of unsold copies and Alfred Harcourt sued the store for loss of sales.

As publishers though, we were still a little leery about material that might be found objectionable. When we published the auto-biography of Dr. Hugh Young, an eminent urologist at the famous Brady clinic at Johns Hopkins, we did a little precautionary editing that puzzled the doctor.

Dr. Young was a specialist in the prostate operation and his most famous patient was Diamond Jim Brady, whom he sent back to Lillian Russell in such good shape that Brady endowed a special clinic at Johns Hopkins.

Young developed several different methods of performing a prostate operation and required patients to fill out post-operative questionnaires for many months to provide evidence on the results of the various methods.

On the way to an autographing session at a bookstore, Dr. Young described the questionnaire to me in detail. One of the questions was, "How have you found this operation has affected your sexual powers?" He told me that one gentleman in his 70's had left this question unanswered for four successive periods.

"I told my nurse to underline the question and write 'please answer' the next time she sent out the form."

The doctor gave me a quick smile. "When this questionnaire came back the next time the man had written his answer: 'I find it takes a good deal longer, but at my age I don't begrudge the time.'"

He said he didn't quite understand why this anecdote had been cut and I couldn't help agreeing with him.

Not all the memorable happenings of 1938 were concerned with books and publishing by any means. In July our son Christopher was born.

11

The following year, 1939, was very complicated. Due to a disagreement over the terms of an apartment lease, we found ourselves with all our furniture but no place to put it. Emily and Christopher spent the summer in Vermont with family, and I spent most of it in the home of Isabel Ely Lord in Brooklyn with Carl Sandburg as a roommate.

The only member of the cast of this summer menage who needs introduction is Isabel Ely Lord—the owner of the house—and her cats. First Isabel: she was a copy editor and known as about the best there was. I'd better identify different kinds of editors. First the plain editor—the one whose job it was to get books for the firm to publish, and work with the author to make an accepted manuscript as good as it could be. The idea was to ask more of the book while it was in manuscript than any reader or reviewer would ask of it after publication. If he or she came across scenes that didn't seem to come off the scene would be brought up for discussion. The editor could say, "This is what the scene means to me. If that's what you want, we'll leave it alone. If that's not the reader reaction you want, let's talk about it." At its best this procedure was a true partnership. A good editor never said, "If I were writing this scene this is the way I'd do it." So in the end it was always the author's book, the way the author wrote it.

So the manuscript went off to the printer and later of course the editor and author got to see galley proofs. These were long single sheets of paper with columns, not pages of type. Theoretically the printer had carefully proofread the galleys to make sure there were no typographical errors, omitted words, and so on. Good printers caught most of these but never all of them. This was up to the author and the editor.

After them came the copy editor. This rare and highly disciplined professional checked facts—in fiction as well as non-fiction. What kind of facts? All the way from making sure that the heroine's eyes didn't change color during the story unless the change was part of the plot, to making sure that the hero didn't arrive at Atlanta airport on an airline that didn't fly to Atlanta. After the facts had been checked, punctuation, word selection and word usage were examined to see if the author was just being careless, didn't know any better, or was making grammatical errors on purpose.

You might think this would be a foolproof system for publishing writing that had no errors. Most of the time it was, but even the best systems have something in common with mice and men.

I had written some promotion copy about a book on the spring list. I ended the blurb with the sentence, "This book fills a much needed gap in the literature of the subject." This immortal sentence was read and approved by the copy editor and the promotion manager. Finally the young woman who was typing a stencil for the multigraph read the sentence and was puzzled by it. She came to me and asked if there wasn't something funny about "a much needed gap." Red was a popular face color for a while in some parts of the office.

I have a feeling that if I had shown that piece of copy to Isabel Lord she wouldn't have spoken to me for days. When I met her in the office she told me of the enormous amount of work it had taken to bring Carl's four volumes of *Abraham Lincoln, The War Years,* to the state it was in at the moment. All the copy had been set and Isabel was working on the long galley proofs. She and Carl had a mountain of work to do together in resolving queries, assembling the illustrative material and checking facts and references for the last time. All of Isabel's reference materials were in her Brooklyn home. The labor would be easier if Carl were to be in her home too. Also, it would be handy if there were a built-in courier to carry important papers back and forth from Brooklyn to Madison Avenue.

Clearly this was a job for me. Carl and I got along well, and Isabel said if Carl could get along with me she probably could too and I could sleep in one of the twin beds in the spare bedroom.

This took care of me but it left my wife, my son, and our furniture on the curb. Isabel said she and Carl never used the dining room so I could put our furniture in with hers. The solution allowed a narrow path from her living room to her kitchen. That took care of the furniture, but it didn't take care of my family.

It turned out that Chris's grandparents in Vermont were eager to give refuge to the homeless woman and her child. There was excellent train service from New York to Rutland and I spent as many weekends with them as I could. We had not yet acquired a car.

Isabel's home on Emerson Place was really half a two-family house. It had a small front hall, a living room, dining room and kitchen on the first floor. At the top of the steep stairway there was a tiny bedroom that contained shelf after shelf of shoe boxes full of thousands of cards of raw notes for the Lincoln biography. Most of the time the room also contained Isabel.

She was a big woman with straggly gray hair and a body that reflected years of sedentary labor. I don't think she knew that she almost always had a burning cigarette in the corner of her mouth. She never seemed to draw on it and paid no attention to the dusting of ashes down the front of her housecoat.

The second floor had a bath and a second small bedroom with twin beds. This was what Isabel called the "spare" bedroom because she slept in the attic. Often during the hot summer nights I would climb to the top step of the narrow steps that led to the attic.

Isabel would be lying in a massive brass bed surrounded by stacks of yellowing pulp magazines: *Westerns, True Adventures, Tales of the Foreign Legion* and others. She was reading by the light of a single unshaded light bulb hanging from somewhere in the darkness above her. The customary cigarette would be drooping from the corner of her mouth while ashes sprinkled down the front of her faded pink negligee. As we talked, Isabel's scarred yellow tomcat would climb the small ladder that led to an open hatch in the roof. Sometimes he would come back after a few screeches and yowls. Other times he wouldn't come home for days. There was a pole to close the hatchway when it rained.

There were other cats in the house too—four or five Siamese with lovely colors and disgusting habits. They appeared to belong, according to Isabel, to the Guatemalan girl who rented a place to sleep somewhere on the second floor. Carl disliked the cats intensely and sometimes carried around a rolled-up newspaper to knock one of them into the left-field stands if he could catch it right. He figured there must be a secret closet where the girl was hiding to escape from immigration officials. One day she and her cats left and were not seen again. She owed Isabel money, but Isabel said it wasn't enough to worry about.

After sidling our way through the furniture storeroom, the three of us had breakfast in the kitchen. Then I'd be off for Manhattan and Carl and Isabel would go to work. When I got back in the late afternoon I'd usually have a batch of material for Carl's attention and I'd put in an hour or so helping sort drawings and possible photographs.

One morning after I had sidled my way into the kitchen for breakfast I saw Isabel bending over the gas range with tears streaming down her face.

I put my hand on her shoulder and asked if there was anything I could do.

"No," she murmured. "No, last night I was working on the assassination sequence and when I woke up this morning all I could think of was that Mr. Lincoln was dead."

Isabel ate her dinner in. Carl and I usually went out, either to one of the Italian restaurants we could walk to, or lots of times we took the subway down to the Borough Hall area and had dinner at a Horn and Hardart's Automat. Carl liked the food as much as I did. During the dog days the Automat was air-conditioned. We could cool off all right, but the cooling system worked by blasting air over an icefield of some kind. Sometimes we wore sweaters to avoid getting pneumonia.

After dinner we'd walk, sometimes through neighborhoods where we heard only Hebrew being spoken and then a half hour later we would stop and watch games of bocce and hear excited Italian voices raised in cheers or curses. Then, of course, there were black enclaves as well as concentrations of ethnic groups from many lands.

Carl was not a man who did much talking for the sake of talking. He was nearly at the end of his major life work and wasn't in the mood for inconsequential words or discussions.

There were only a few rainy evenings that whole long, dry summer. These Carl and I spent in the living room. Carl would get his guitar and we'd sing folk songs and he'd tell me where he had picked them up.

He made several trips back to Harbert, Michigan to visit his home and family. His wife Mary raised goats on the farm as well as garden produce. She made goat's milk cheese that was strong and wonderfully flavored. He always brought me one or two cheese sandwiches on his return trip. After a day and a half in a hot suitcase on a hot train the sandwiches were very fragrant indeed.

There were two narrow beds in the spare bedroom. Carl didn't snore and he never said that I did. One night he suddenly sat up in bed, called to me and said, "We shouldn't have killed those two men." Then he sank back on his pillow and in the morning remembered nothing about his words.

One night we were talking about Alfred Harcourt for whom Carl felt great admiration and affection. He remarked that the only thing he could never understand about Alfred was the look of glee that came over his face when he won a ping pong game.

Several nights later I went along with Carl to the Pennsylvania Station in New York where he was taking a train to spend the weekend with a friend of his who was the president of Union Carbide. I asked Carl what the man was like and he replied, "He'd be a rich man without his millions."

The following day I was having lunch with my boss Hastings Harcourt, and Alfred came to the table and asked if he could join us. He sat down and asked about Carl. I reported on Carl's health and the excellent progress on the book. Then, for no reason at all, I told him what Carl had said about the president of Union Carbide.

Alfred smiled. "I never knew anyone who could sum up a man in one phrase as well as Carl can."

Hastings and I managed to agree while keeping straight faces, but I don't know how.

The following year, 1940, marked the birth of our second son and further involvement on my part with the editorial and promotion departments.

More and more frequently I was given advance galleys of books that would be on our next list and asked to give my guess as to what kind of sales they might have. One of these was called *Mrs. Miniver.* It was a collection of essays and sketches written by an Englishwoman about life in England during the early days of World War II. Jan Struther's essays and poems had been frequently published in England and several of the poems were often set to music in the hymnal of the Episcopal Church.

All the editors agreed that it was a very nice little book that probably would have a suitably modest sale.

I read it and loved it. I found it beautifully written, simple and extremely moving. I sent the galleys up to my mother who read it and called up with tearful enthusiasm of the highest order. That was all my salesman's instinct needed. Seeing no reason to curb my zeal, the next time I met Alfred Harcourt in the hall I expressed my belief in the book's future. He was pleased. He knew very well what it meant to have a salesman who was this worked up over a book. He asked me how many copies I thought the book was going to sell.

"A quarter of a million," I said.

He didn't want to dampen my ardor, but he did say that he thought it might well not come anywhere near that figure. I asked him if he'd give me 100-1 odds that it didn't. For a dollar.

The wager was accepted. About a year later I got a check from

Alfred and a specially bound edition of *Mrs. Miniver* with the words "Two Hundred and Fifty Thousandth Copy" stamped in gold on the cover. In 1942 William Wyler directed a big movie, made from the little book, which won four Oscars including best picture.

Horace Liveright, one of the most colorful of American book publishers during the 1920's, was said to give a good deal of weight to readings of manuscripts by his elevator man and janitor. I don't remember seeking a response from my mother on any other book, but I learned to place a lot of confidence in readings by my wife—especially in her spasms of delight over *The Education of Hyman Kaplan* and *My Sister Eileen.*

Jan Struther's book had been published in England before we printed an American edition so Jan did not have an editor here to consult with. This pleasant role fell upon the sales and promotion departments, and I guess she felt easy with me because I liked her book so much and she knew about the bet.

Jan was an unassuming woman with a slight, strong figure and, at first sight, a face that was not much more than pleasant looking. But as you got to know her you were captivated by the light of impish humor in her eyes and the mischievous quality of her quick smiles.

Emily, an anglophile of high degree, suggested we ask Jan out to our new apartment for dinner because she probably didn't have all that many friends in New York. I thought that a fine idea and when I asked her she said she'd love to come. We set a date, Emily went to work on the menu, and I got a bottle of sherry in case she didn't like martinis or Scotch on the rocks.

I got home early from the office and Emily greeted me with a look of such happy anticipation that I thought she must have won the Irish sweepstakes.

"Jan Struther called," she said.

"Yes." I waited.

"She asked if she could bring a friend."

"And you said, 'of course,' because you just happened to have enough dinner."

She nodded. "Don't you want to know who the friend is?"

"Male or female?" I asked.

"Male."

"Do I know him?"

"Yes and no," Emily said. "You've seen him in the movies."

"I give up, who?"

"Roland Young. Isn't that wonderful?"

It was wonderful too. He was one of our favorite actors. We had loved him in every movie we had seen him in. Particularly perhaps his playing of the most attractive English Lord in *Ruggles of Red Gap* and his masterly performance as the loathsome Uriah Heep in *David Copperfield.*

We both felt a little apprehensive. A bestselling author and a ranking movie star were coming for dinner. Our apartment was not spacious and the dining room was not a room at all, just an extension of the kitchen furnished with a plank harvest table with benches on both sides. We certainly weren't ashamed of it, but we did think it would be quite a change from the way our guests were usually entertained.

When the knock on the door finally came we opened the door together to find Jan on the threshold. We did not see her escort for another moment; then Roland appeared riding a child's tricycle that he had found at our neighbor's door. His whole face was crinkled in a smile of infinite glee.

While we were drinking cocktails, conversation didn't lag, but it didn't sparkle either. I began to worry about how to steer our table talk during dinner—if it needed steering.

We put Jan and Roland on the bench against the dinette wall, Emily served the plates and we began to eat.

After a while Jan began to speak in a desultory way about religious life in some of the small English towns she knew. She described the rectors and rectories and the old, small churches. Emily was fascinated. She had not yet made her first trip to England and it seemed only natural that Jan Struther, the poet and writer of hymns, should talk about churchly matters.

Then Jan said she'd like to tell a story about a minister and his wife who went to inspect the rectory and the church of the parish to which he had recently been assigned. The gardener was showing the couple around the lovely, neat borders and the artfully planted flower beds when an upstairs window opened and the hidden audience heard the voice of the gardener's wife.

Jan paused, tantalized us with a smile "She called down, 'Albert,

I've just come up to put meself tidy. Shall you want to use me before I put me drawers on?'"

After that I had no worries about steering the dinner conversation. The bottle of sherry remained unopened. We fell to drinking Scotch on the rocks. It was a very companionable evening.

That fall we brought down a girl from Vermont who had been working for my mother during the summer. Lucilla was one of a group of disadvantaged girls (probably abused) rescued by the Episcopal Church and given an education as well as some training in domestic work. Our responsibility was to give her a home and guidance and pay her the most minimum of wages. She was a great help, especially with the boys.

Emily did the cooking, but Lucilla did the cleaning up and it turned out that somehow she had learned to make a chocolate bread pudding that was a gastronomic miracle.

The dessert was too good to keep to ourselves. We asked Jan out for dinner again. This time she brought Artie Shaw. Shy little friendless Englishwoman indeed.

Emily and I were overjoyed. Lucilla was in ecstasy and almost collapsed under Artie's expressions of rapture over her chocolate bread pudding.

This was one of the best times with Jan. We played some of Artie's recordings on the big old record player and tried not to talk about the war, but that was impossible. Dunkirk...the Battle of Britain...the bombing of London... the passage of the American Selective Service Act...it was too much. We knew it was our war, too, and before long we would be actively engaged in it.

The next time Artie came out he brought with him a recording of his newest composition, "Concerto for Clarinet." We thought it was a beautifully wrought and very exciting composition. One movement began with a deep drum pattern followed by the voice of Artie's clarinet in a low register.

When we had played it twice I commented that the rhythm of drums and the song of the clarinet reminded me of American Indian tribal music.

Artie looked at me pityingly, "Didn't you ever hear a cantor?"

Of course we had the famous dessert—and a good thing too, because Artie said that was all he came out for. When he left he wrote a note in Lucilla's autograph book:

> Roses are red
> Violets are blue
> Sugar is sweet
> And you make a hell of a bread pudding.

We saw each other occasionally over the next ten years and I met several of his beautiful, talented wives. He had a restless, questing mind and I always urged him to write his autobiography.

Carl Sandburg's *Abraham Lincoln: The War Years* was published and won the Pulitzer Prize. Ernest Hemingway's *For Whom the Bell Tolls* was published and didn't. For some occult reason the Pulitzer Prize for fiction was given to John Steinbeck's stunning *Grapes of Wrath* which had been published the year before.

Hemingway's publishers, Charles Scribner's Sons, were shocked. Apparently they had been given to believe the prize was going to their author.

The Scribner Bookstore on Fifth Avenue dramatized the event by draping one of their two great display windows in black with a small square exhibiting a single copy of *For Whom the Bell Tolls*.

One of the more colorful characters at Scribner's Bookstore was Dave Randall—the rare book specialist, and a famous one.

Listening to David tell stories about the rare book business and some of its more piratical dealers was like hearing tales of such venality as to put the Medicis to shame. After David had finished one such story I asked him how the value of a rare book or manuscript which had not been sold before was established.

"Anything you can get for it." For the record David was both direct and honest.

"For instance, in one carton of jumbled manuscripts I bought at a Massachusetts country auction I found a holograph manuscript of an unknown short story by Nathaniel Hawthorne. I put it in my briefcase and took the next train for Cincinnati."

"Why Cincinnati?"

"Because that was where my richest Hawthorne collector lived. Anyway, when the train left Penn Station I began to read the story. By the time we got to Trenton I figured the story was worth five thousand dollars. I kept thinking about it and when we pulled into Philadelphia I knew it was worth a lot more...ten, fifteen thousand. Just before I went to sleep near

Pittsburgh I figured the lowest I could get for it was twenty."

It was my turn. "What finally happened in Cincinnati?"

David grinned. "When I met with my man he asked me how much it was going to cost him and I said, 'twenty-five thousand dollars.' He wrote me a check on the spot."

"Did he ask you how you arrived at the price since it had never been published or sold before?"

"I told him the whole story," David said, "and when I finished he looked at me and said, 'I'm lucky I don't live in San Francisco.'"

13

By the time Franklin Roosevelt was inaugurated for his third term we all knew we were going to war. The question was, what role would each of us take in it. The publishing business began detailed discussions of its responsibilities and began to estimate what shortages would show up in the various materials that went into the manufacture of books as well as what part books could play in the total war effort.

On the whole, business went on more or less as usual at HB. I had the exciting experience of having my first book published. I became an author instead of a writer and felt all the reactions I had witnessed, and in many cases deplored, in other authors. The book got wide and astonishing critical praise, but some publications didn't like it much and others didn't review it at all. The advertising budget was meager, the advance sales were not promising and not a single bookstore pressed for an autographing party. As the months went by it became apparent that the publisher had a lot of other books to worry about and plan for. I had learned a lot about authors by becoming one.

Incidentally, the book was published by Harcourt Brace and Company. The year before, I had finally found a way to present Vermont humor in combination with genre photographs that I thought would work. I talked to A.H. about it and he said it wouldn't.

During an early vacation in Vermont Emily and I made a dummy of the book—pictures and all. When I showed the dummy to A.H. he looked through it in an unbelieving sort of way and said,

"It will sweep the country."

I had a contract the next day. The book was titled *Vermont Is Where You Find It* and it didn't sweep the country, but it has been in print for over fifty years.

Six months before, the head of the College Textbook department had shown me a multigraphed manuscript that was being used in class by the University of Chicago professor S.I. Hayakawa. The text was called *"Language in Action."* Someone in his department had recalled that I had been interested in this subject and I was asked to read it and say whether or not the trade sales department might be justified in offering an edition to the general reading public.

I read it and rejoiced over its simplicity and clarity. I already had an amateur's enthusiasm for the complex subjects of linguistics and semantics and was enormously grateful for the new perceptions that the book gave me. Chase's *The Tyranny of Words* had done well, but I felt that this book would appeal more directly to the immediate self- interest of the reading public and so I recommended it most energetically to the trade department.

In due course the book was published and to everyone's surprise, including mine, was taken by the Book-of-the-Month Club and became a bestseller.

The Harcourt editors were wonderful to work with. When I was given galley proofs of a book called *The Bombing of Britain* or something equally uninviting, I found it full of action and human interest, but I thought narrative elements were all out of order. The editors challenged me to cut up the galleys and re-arrange the content and give it a title I liked better. I did just that and named the story *Journey for Margaret.* My version was published and later on Bob Giroux, with his customary generosity, said that I had made the book a bestseller.

There was some talk about my cutting down on my sales territories and spending more time in the office but I discouraged the discussion. It seemed to me I was learning too much from being close to booksellers not only in Manhattan but throughout New England as well. But this was just a small part of the book market in the country.

I was not trying to calculate the book needs of the mass entertainment market; I wanted experience to help me identify the special audiences for books I believed to be of lasting value. I had learned early that if you publish a book for everybody it usually turns out to be for nobody.

Usually the big accounts in the Middle West were handled out of the New York office by the sales manager. The West Coast and the South were covered by commission salesmen who represented several publishers. I met the HB commission salesmen a couple of times a year at the time of our sales conferences. Wilbur Goubeaud was our man in the South, and at one conference he told of a peculiar happening in Atlanta.

"The hotel had published my name and business connection, and when I got to my room there was a message from an Atlanta lady who asked if I could please make a personal business call at her home. I called and made the appointment."

Wilbur paused to encourage speculation as to what kind of traveling salesman story this was going to be. Then he went on,

"I went to her house and knocked on the door, gave my name and was invited in. The lady sat down on the couch, reached down and pulled up her skirt about six inches above her knee. She pointed at the knee and said, 'This is where it hurts.'"

Wilbur said he asked her what she meant and she told him again that the pain was in her knee. He explained that there wasn't anything he could do about it.

"She gave me a very funny look," Wilbur continued, and said, "but aren't you from the Harcourt Brace Company?"

Wilbur confirmed that he did indeed represent Harcourt Brace and Company but what he sold wouldn't help her knee.

A few months later I couldn't say I represented Harcourt Brace and Company because I didn't. I had been fired.

For reasons that are not significant now—and may never have been—Helen Taylor and I were responsible for a memorandum to A.H. which contained critical comments on a member of the management. We thought, at the time, that it was for the good of the firm but, since we were both instantly fired, it could have been judged only as an act of mutiny.

Helen decided to leave publishing and become a professional photographer, a career for which she was admirably qualified. I began to look for another job.

In the weeks that followed, many of our friends at HB sent us messages of support and encouragement. There was no great period of uncertainty and worry, because before Pearl Harbor and the end of the year I was offered, and took, the job of Sales Manager of the Trade Department of Henry Holt and Company.

When I went to work for Henry Holt and Company the trade department of that venerable house was enjoying a renaissance under the direction of the talented, energetic William Sloane. He had devised a new setting for the jewel in Holt's publishing crown—Robert Frost, who claimed to be perfectly satisfied with his publisher for the first time in many years.

When I try to view the incidents of the next two years, it is something like watching a videotape set on fast forward. The department was small and everybody worked at everything. Bill wanted the best for our books—in selection, editing, design, manufacture, promotion and sales. And he made us all want it as much as he did. He is remembered as one of the most brilliant book publishing editors of his time and was the author of two classic science fiction novels. His literary interests ranged from the award-winning *American Men of Letters* series to the best contemporary poetry he could find. He spent time with D.J.B. Rhine in the early studies of ESP and published the controversial and stimulating *There is a River* by Edgar Cayce. He served actively on the Council on Books in Wartime, the Armed Services Editions and was on the faculty of the Breadloaf Writers' conference. He had a long list of things that mattered and cared deeply about all of them.

In my first two years as sales manager I had two-million-copy books which made life very pleasurable indeed. The first of these was *See Here Private Hargrove* by Marion Hargrove.

The book had come to Bill from the hands of Maxwell Anderson, his friend and neighbor on South Mountain Road in Rockland Country north of Nyack, New York. Max had accepted the collection of accounts of the life of a draftee in basic training at Fort Bragg during an official visit to the Fort.

Bill read it, bought it and published it without drawing breath. The book was an instantaneous and mushrooming bestseller. For the first time in my life I ordered reprints by the carload—of paper. A carload would print 55,000 copies.

Marion was a soft-spoken North Carolinian with a gift for telling stores of humorous happenings in the lives of young Americans being trained for battle that were both touching and wildly funny. He came to New York off and on and often stayed with us in Jackson Heights. He was dating a stunningly lovely girl who was either Miss Rheingold—the Poster Queen—or about to become Miss Rheingold. At some point during the evenings they spent with us the young lady would call her mother and ask me to say hello. I could assume only that this came under the heading of chaperone certification.

Marion seemed to like the idea of being part of a family. He went so far as to take Chris and Nick out to the play yard and make up games for them to play. On one memorable day he took them both to the Bronx Zoo. After the war he moved close to us in Rockland County.

Our list was a salesman's dream. We published an impressive little book, *Democratic Ideals* and Reality by Sir Halford Mackinder, a book which introduced American readers to the geopolitical concepts that colored Hitler's dreams of world conquest.

A modest self-help book called *A Mathematics Refresher* went through printing after printing. The whole list sold well and reflected Bill Sloane's editorial acumen.

It took me a good many months to be comfortable with becoming part of management. People came to me for decisions I was used to pushing along for someone else to make. I had new sales policies to make and new salesmen's territories to define. Naturally I kept the best and biggest accounts for myself.

No one of us who ever sold Chicago will forget The Argus Bookshop and Ben Abramson. Ben specialized in the books of contemporary English and American writers who were already, or about to become, famous. His shop, on the second floor of a building on North Michigan Avenue, was a haven for writers he knew and liked: Ben Hecht, Charles McArthur, Carl Sandburg, and others whose names I have inexcusably forgotten. He published a book letter that went out all over the country and helped many writers toward recognition and sales.

His shop was a huge, double-height room with books on three walls and a picture window facing Lake Michigan on the fourth. A steep, small staircase on one wall led up to a mysterious room which I finally learned Ben used for stocking not only books that were banned in most civilized countries, but also contained a desk and a typewriter where his needy author friends could write pornographic tales for customers with special reading needs.

On one visit, I've forgotten what year it was but it was at the height of the rationing program, Ben and I were standing at the big window watching traffic when we saw a barrel fall off the back of an overloaded truck. The barrel rolled into the gutter just below us, the truck went on its way and nobody paid any attention to the barrel. After a few minutes Ben suggested we go down and see what was in it.

On one end stenciled letters identified its contents as lanolin. Ben wasn't quite sure what lanolin was used for, but we figured it must be valuable so we almost broke our backs trundling the barrel inside the door that led to the stairs up to Ben's store.

About a year later I was visiting Ben again and asked him what had happened about the barrel. Did somebody track it down and claim it, or what?

Ben gave me a conspirator's smile. "No, nobody came for it so I had it brought up here. Lanolin is, and I quote, a fatty substance obtained from wool. So I tried to find out what it was used for. After quite a search I discovered it was the key ingredient in products used for leather preservatives."

Now a bigger and more conspiratorial smile. "So I wrote to the Department of Commerce and they sent me some material that contained a formula for making a leather preservative."

Knowing Ben, I began to see what was coming. "So I got the rest of the stuff I needed and made a dozen bottles of what I advertised as Ye Olde Argus Bookshop Famous Leather Preservative. One of the first requests was from the Library of Congress who said they wanted to try it out."

Ben paused, "You wouldn't believe what happened."

"Oh, yes I would."

"I got an order from them for 500 bottles."

"Why that's great," I said.

"Sure," Ben said, "but I needed a lot more lanolin and when I tried to order it I was told it was strictly rationed and I would need authorization from the War Department."

"Let me guess," I said, "so you wrote the War Department for priority because the Library of Congress needed it—and they gave it to you."

"You got it," Ben said. "So there I was making my famous old leather preservative from a formula from the Department of Commerce for the Library of Congress with cooperation from the War Department."

All this simply confirmed my theory that if you want to know how to get something done—ask a bookseller. If they weren't talented improvisation experts they probably wouldn't have gone into the retail book business in the first place.

There were great moments in all the bookstores in most of the cities I went to. One such, which has a hallowed place in the folklore of book salesmen, took place in St. Louis, at a leading department store—Stix, Baer and Fuller. The book department was on the ground floor and on the memorable day was crowded by members of the St. Louis Cardinals baseball team—in uniform—celebrating the publication of the most recent book on that great ball club.

The book was selling furiously, players were autographing copies of the book and baseballs, too. The buyer, Lillian Friedman, one of everybody's favorite buyers, was in her office on the balcony looking down on this exciting scene when she was told the stock of baseballs was used up and more were needed at once.

Lil called her sporting goods department and asked them to send down a few more dozen. In ten minutes they were delivered to Lillian in her office.

Not wanting to lose a single sales moment, she grabbed the microphone of her storewide PA system and made her announcement.

"Anyone who wants his balls autographed come to Miss Friedman's office on the balcony."

There was a moment of silence and then the store exploded.

Between trips I worked at my office duties, wrote some draft advertising and promotion copy and read a lot of manuscripts.

As a result of the success of the books we published, more and more manuscripts were sent to us for consideration. The editorial load increased and it was clear we needed another editor. Helen Taylor had done some fine work for the Harcourt editorial department and I thought she might just be the editor we needed at Holt.

I asked her to come and talk to Bill and some others of our group. Bill offered Helen the job and after careful thought Helen took it. It was good to work closely with her again.

It wasn't long before we had another big, war-book bestseller. On the train going to work every morning I read *The New York Times.* One morning I began to read a story on the front page that told of the incredible triumph of three Navy fliers whose plane went down in the Pacific. They had survived for thirty-four days on a four-by eight-foot rubber raft. With no supplies or equipment they had somehow managed to reach an inhabited atoll about a thousand miles from where their plane had gone down. The story, signed by a Robert Trumbull, was written with the kind of evocative simplicity that marked the best of Hemingway's work for the *Toronto Star.*

"Got to be a wonderful book here," I thought and got off the train at the next stop, hoping that other publishers would wait until they got to the office, have a meeting, and then inquire about book rights. Taking advantage of my new executive status, I sent a telegram to Trumbull saying Henry Holt and Company wanted to publish his book on the adventures of the three men and that we would call him later in the day.

When I met Bill in the office I told him about my telegram. He read the story and reached for his telephone. He was so eager to confirm an agreement that I had to remind him of the time difference between New York and Honolulu.

Bob Trumbull wrote us an outstanding book, entitled *The Raft,* that was hailed as "the most inspiring story the war had produced," compared to Conrad, taken by the Book-of-the-Month Club and climbed high on the bestseller lists.

Robert Frost didn't come to the office very often, but I usually saw him when he did and his being so happy with Bill made him also content with my company. Thinking back, I have a hunch that our friendship was based, to some extent, on the fact that we had both loved *The Prisoner of Zenda* when we were kids. He was a strange, prickly man who often said things he didn't mean, and sometimes things that were just mean.

After visiting him at Ripton, Vermont one fall Bill told me that he was standing with Robert near the woodpile while Robert was splitting chunks for stove wood.

A slender young man with flowing hair and garments came drifting down past them through the trees. He passed without speaking. Bill said, "I asked Robert who he was and what he did." Robert tossed some split wood on the pile and said,

"He doesn't do anything, he's a poet."

We were doing very well indeed with war-related books, but I wondered if there might not be a substantial readership for a good historical kind of novel that let readers live for a while in a more peaceful time. With the help of a bookseller, I finally did find a book I thought might attract this kind of reader.

The Harry Marks Bookstore was a Park Avenue establishment that specialized in rare editions and fine bindings. It was not a bookstore that carried the kind of books I had been selling, but I loved to go in when I had time and feast on the sight of so many books bound in the finest of leathers and stamped with the heaviest of gold foil. Once in a while I would find Mr. Marks in command, but most of the time I would talk with the attractive, knowledgeable Harriet Munro. We were talking one day about current books and I remember saying they were mostly all very serious and learned and important, but there didn't seem to much around to be read just for the sheer enjoyment of reading.

Harriet said that the best book of the kind she thought I was talking about had been published a couple of years before in a limited edition. She produced a beautifully made volume titled *Bolinvar.* I opened it to page one and read the first sentence. To the best of my recollection the sentence read, "It was the spring of Waterloo, I was just down from the gentlemen's college at Princeton and I was as lean and fit as a panther." (I may have a word or so wrong.)

I bought a copy of the book, read it and thought it was exactly what I had been looking for. I won't say that my colleagues were as happy with it as I was. It certainly wasn't "literature" and would win no prizes. But I was convinced that it was a book that would give many readers a wonderful time.

The Derrydale Press gave us the last-known address of the

author, Marguerite Bayliss, but finding her was complicated. It turned out that she had been declared incompetent and was a ward of the State of New Jersey. She was also penniless. Finally our lawyer arranged a contract, we paid an advance to the author and added the book to our spring list.

By the time the reviewers had a chance to write about it, the book had been taken by a book club and was in its second printing before publication.

I won't even sketch the plot, which involved handsome cousins, great horses, foxhunts, and hounds whose baying was in the same class with epic music.

The New York Times wrote of the book, "Mrs. Bayliss' tale of bravery, strength and chivalry will carry the reader far away from a mechanized age of war and terror."

The New Yorker, in a review that is one of my all-time favorites, wrote, "The book will undoubtedly be enjoyed by those who don't want to think about the war; it will be enjoyed even more by those who don't want to think at all."

Somehow the success of the book, and the income from it, made Mrs. Bayliss legally competent. She came to the office a few times beautifully dressed in a tweed suit and flowing cape, voluble, enthusiastic and grateful. The last we heard of her she had taken to raising horses in southern Vermont. Years later I searched for her in the Bennington area, but she had left without a trace.

In late October 1942, 400,000 American troops landed in French North Africa. Weeks later a Scripps-Howard correspondent's columns were running in hundreds of American newspapers. The correspondent's name was Ernie Pyle. He wrote not about grand strategy but about how the boys were doing.

We published a collection of Ernie's columns under the title *Here is Your War.* It was our second million-copy seller in two years. I've never been quite sure how Bill managed to obtain the book rights from Lee Miller, the Scripps-Howard editor who, he said, had been made vice-President in charge of Pyle.

While the book was still in the making Bill went to China on a several months' assignment from a semi-secret branch of government to gauge what was going on there. Later, Bill published the papers of "Vinegar Joe" Stillwell and a marvelous book, *Thunder Out of China* by Theodore White and Anna Lee Jacoby, so the trip was hardly a waste of time. The trip made me the Vice-President in charge of Pyle for Henry Holt, and it was a great assignment.

When Ernie was summoned home, not for new instructions in the diplomats' term, but, according to Lee Miller, to keep him from working himself to death, I went down to Washington to spend some time with him.

Ernie was a slightly built, slow and soft-spoken man, who invited more confidences than he gave. He was interested in everything about people, avoided talking about himself, but talked fluently on matters that really ignited him. Take language, for instance.

Like all fine artists Ernie had the greatest respect for his materials. And, of course, his materials were words. One night he was holding forth on the word fuck. "It didn't bother me at first," he said, "but then the GI's began to use it two or three times in every sentence. Just as soon as I more or less got used to that they began to interpolate it in phrases, like 'I have to get up at six a fuckin' clock in the morning'."

I asked him how he would spell the word if he had to use it. He thought for an instant and said he thought maybe he'd forget about "g". "It's never sounded anyway."

Then he laughed and said he had heard one four-word sentence in which the word was used three times.

"We came across a GI trying to kick a motorcycle to pieces that was lying flat on the ground. I asked him what his problem was."

"He looked up and snarled, 'The fuckin' fucker's fucked.'"

After another ten minutes of how this word was dominating all conversation Ernie signed off by saying, "Sometimes I think if I ever hear that word used as an adjective again I'll cut my fuckin' throat."

As far as I remember the first novel that really reported the language of our soldiers accurately was *The Naked and the Dead,* Norman Mailer's great manuscript about the GI's in the Pacific. From the first page the word appeared in the majority of the dialogue lines. Mailer knew perfectly well that while some readers might resent this, after another ten pages the word would have lost its shock and become acceptable in its context.

However, the book was owned by Farrar and Rinehart and their editors had a problem with the word. They felt that the great American reading public wasn't quite ready to see that awful word in print. Further, the Rinehart brothers were perfectly sure their mother, the famous bestselling novelist Mary Roberts Rinehart, never would be.

Consequently, when the first printing arrived in bookstores the word was spelled "fuggin." An unfortunate solution because the counterfeit word called attention to itself every time it was used.

The book was an immediate smash hit and at a party celebrating its triumph Norman Mailer was introduced to one of the ranking celebrities of the day, a certain Miss Tallulah Bankhead. Miss Bankhead smiled at him, her famous liquid eyes glowing, and said, "Oh yes, you're the young man who doesn't know how to spell fuck."

All this furor about a perfectly good old Anglo-Saxon word which meant "to prepare a field for seeding by making holes in it with a pointed pole" brought me back to the consideration of what my own standards were. For a long time, in literary circles, I had heard the words "belles- lettres" used to define a category of books. But I had never known just what the category was. *The Reader's Encyclopedia* wasn't much help. "Polite literature; poetry and standard literary works which are not scientific or technical."

Well, at least I knew one kind of salesman/editor/ publisher I was not. I couldn't imagine condemning any book because it wasn't polite. I knew what kind of writing I liked, what kind of story-telling and character drawing impressed me. I was grateful to books that gave me a good time and gave me new insights into people and the worlds they lived in.

It seemed to me that there wasn't much point in worrying about what level brow I was. I had read and re-read many "classics" that I had liked and quite a few that I had started, several times, and never finished. I agreed with some critics' opinions and not with others and was always amused when one of our books would get rave reviews from some and offered to the garbage heap by others.

Over the years I got to know many of the critics and can say, like Will Rogers, I never met one I didn't like. We entertained many of them at parties given for a new author, or a well known one, enjoyed their company and if they gave bad reviews to the guest of honor we never asked for our martinis back.

Somehow a manuscript grew in stature during the publishing process. Once a manuscript had been accepted, perhaps after much disagreement, it was agreed to be a very good book indeed. Our rule was to publish only very good books, therefore this must be one. During the editing process it got better still. When we picked words to describe its qualities for our catalog description the book's quality climaxed. When we wrote copy for the jacket flaps to impress the browser that this was just the book he was looking for, the book became irresistible. Sometimes I felt that we had gone too far, but what was the alternative? Wasn't it better to let the damning with faint praise be done by our friends the critics?

Only once during a book's   prepublication life is there ever unanimity of opinion as to its great merit. This moment occurs during the semi-annual sales conference when it is presented by its editor to the house salesmen and commission men who will offer it to booksellers.

These carefully orchestrated and choreographed productions were usually presented in one of the meeting rooms of a convenient hotel. Coffee had to be available all day long, and other liquids at the midday break. We usually sat at a long, wide table with the top executives at one end, editors and salesmen along the sides and whoever was in charge of the proceedings at the other end.

The books to be published in the following season were presented one by one to the sales force. The idea, naturally, was to inspire the salesmen to get at least a few copies of every book into every bookstore they called on and appropriately larger quantities to the key regional booksellers.

The trick was for the conductor to see to it that no editor used an unfair amount of time on his or her pet books. At the end of the day there were always remarks about how certain books had not been adequately dealt with. The comments were always directed to the conductor, or the ringmaster or whoever was running the show. For many years I did this job. Perhaps because I felt the editorial commitment just as much as the sales responsibility.

Very few American lives were untouched by the war in 1943. Wages were frozen; meat, cheese, fats and all canned foods were rationed. Publishers' paper quotas forced many compromises in book design and numbers of copies printed. Some titles under contract were indefinitely postponed.

Robert Frost's *A Witness Tree* won a Pulitzer Prize and Ernie Pyle's *Here Is Your War* was an instant and giant bestseller. Henry Holt and Company published another of my picture and text books which wasn't.

Early in 1944 I was drafted. I went through the processing procedure, was okayed and proceeded to a check point where I was asked if I preferred the Army or the Navy. I said Army. My file was stamped Navy. I asked about the Marine Corps and was told that at my advanced age I would have to go back for additional physical examinations. I went back and was okayed for the Marine Corps and given a date to report. I was surprised that the date was more than a month away. I supplied my writing and publishing background to a placement office of the Corps and was ticketed as a combat correspondent—after I had finished my training at Parris Island—an experience I dreaded.

So we made plans. Emily would have to take the boys to Vermont where the grandparents were again ready to shelter and cherish them. I closed down my office at Holt—with the commitment that I would have it back when I got the war over with.

I was given a farewell lunch in a private dining room of the Gramercy Park Hotel, which was kind of sad for a while until the management suddenly turned on the Muzak system and the sound of soaring violin music flooded the room. We all broke into laughter and had a good time.

Within days I received a letter from my draft board telling me that a whole class of New York State fathers of my age with two children had been drafted by mistake and I was to forget about military service. The letter didn't even suggest that I volunteer.

Almost before I had a chance to consider what my next step would be I had a telephone call from a publishing friend who had helped with the early organization of The Office of War

Information. He asked if it were true that I was at liberty at the moment, having been excused by the Marine Corps, and if it was true would I have lunch with him the following day.

At lunch he told me about an OWI program called The Information Centers. These were to be collections of research materials on developments in the fields of history, science, the arts, politics, economics—all the news that had been denied the occupied countries in Europe since the Nazi conquests. These materials were to be fitted into wooden file boxes designed to fit in an Army weapons carrier. The plan was that full loads of these materials would be delivered to liberated cities on the continent as soon as possible after the Allied forces had moved along on their drive to Berlin.

These materials would be made available to newspapers and magazines who would be free to publish but had had no access to information from the outside world for five years.

My friend said the program was already under way. File boxes had been delivered to the Information Center warehouse in England. Library technicians had been recruited to keep the collections current as additional material arrived from the States. All the program needed was a director to be based in London, keep track of the different pieces of the operation and work with the Army to see that things went as they should. The job of director was open and did I want it.

I asked him how much time I had to make a decision and he said not much. It seemed to be to be a sensible, valuable and very contributive program. My family had already made some unhappy adjustments to my joining the Marine Corps, and when I talked over this new job with Emily she listened with a growing sense of relief.

So I went down to Washington for indoctrination, met Elmer Davis who was running the whole show and whom I had admired for years, was introduced to so many bureaucratic procedures that I wondered how any federal agency ever got anything done, was sent out to a camp on Long Island for physical training—nothing like Parris Island, and finally was given a departure date.

I boarded one of the great Pan American Clippers in Jamaica Bay and my first impression was that there was no way this building was going to get off the water, much less fly to Ireland. I had a comfortable bed and a glorious trip. From Shannon our small group was taken across Northern Ireland by bus. It was a rainy morning and I was saddened by the desolate little towns we went through with poorly dressed children walking barefoot to school over the cold cobblestones.

We were delivered to an unnamed airstrip on the east coast of Ireland and flown, blacked-out, to an unidentified airfield in Southern England. We went into London aboard a small bus and for the first time I heard the sound of the V-l bombs.

We all had read about the Battle of Britain and the massive German air raids on London and, in a way, I was heartened to see so many of the great buildings still standing. I guess I had envisioned a city in ruins. There were terrible signs of damage everywhere but not what I had foreseen.

I was delivered to an overnight lodging in a building close to the Marble Arch and got my first lesson in how to adjust to living during a plague of buzz bombs. When you first heard the rising and falling scream of the sirens you stopped whatever you were doing and listened. Soon you heard the sound of a poor quality motorcycle engine somewhere up there in the sky above you. The noise would get louder—up to a point—then stop. Three or four seconds later you would hear the sound of the explosion as the bomb hit. The rule was this: if you heard the sound of the motor begin to decrease, you could forget it—it wasn't going to hit anywhere near you. On the other hand, if the motor cut off while the sound was increasing, you took action. Exactly what action depended on where you were. Crouching under a desk or table was an accepted practice. Sliding under a bed, if one was handy, was another. Closets weren't bad if you had time to get into one and shut the door. If you could cram yourself into any space under a stairway you were in the best place of all.

In buildings with many windows, chards of glass driven by the bomb's blast did the most damage to people. The path that bomb blast took was utterly inexplicable. It would take out the fronts of houses on one side of a street and leave the houses on the other side untouched. It would jump completely over a whole row of houses and savage the houses in the next block.

My secretary was bombed out of an apartment twice during the months I was in London. The first time, she was not at home and her flat was demolished. The second time, she was staying with a friend and sleeping in an overstuffed arm chair that could be easily converted into a bed. The seat pulled out and the back could be raised to make room for the sleeper's head. The bomb hit close and the windows were all blown in or drawn out. Nancy told me that once she felt like moving she had to push up the seat of the chair which had fallen down on her head.

Up to that moment she had been standing in front of my desk explaining why she was late coming to work. Then her voice began to quaver and she sat down.

"When I stood up and looked down at the chair there were six or seven triangles of glass sticking into the cushion that had been over my face."

Later she told me that nothing else in her friend's flat had been damaged except that a glass splinter had somehow pierced a jar of marmalade safely stored behind closed pantry doors. She said she knew that was impossible, but there it was.

On my first day in London I met all the OWI people I would be dealing with, and after lunch, was shown the way to the Center's office on North Audley Street.

At lunch I met Harold Guinzburg, a man I was to admire and respect for the rest of my life. Harold was the president of the Viking Press, a publishing firm he had founded in 1925 and which had attracted a staff of distinguished editors and former publishers whose standards of excellence were not surpassed in the industry. Harold was a gentleman, as well as the successful owner of interests of far more magnitude than the Viking Press. But his heart was in publishing.

Harold's relationship to the OWI was a loose one. He was close to all the Washington people who had designed it and gave it all the time and dedication he could take away from his beloved publishing company. He liked the Information Center program, and I was to see a good deal of him both in London and Paris in the following months.

The staff of the Center program were attractive, youngish men and women who had library training, and whose job it was to catalogue and pack the information materials as they arrived from the States and keep everything as current as possible.

My job was to keep the process going as planned and to keep my superiors advised as to the exact state of our readiness. The former was not hard. The people were dedicated and serious and were willing to work whatever strange hours were necessary, either in London or in the warehouse in Cambridge.

The latter proved to be frustrating. Every week there was a meeting of division heads in a conference room at Inveresk House, with our Ambassador Winant in attendance. Some of our units were ready to move out by the time I got to London. Every week I would report how many more units were ready to be put to the use they had been created for, and every week I was told to be patient. American forces were advancing toward Paris and they had passed through many cities which could have used our information files. Every time I brought this up I was told, as the weeks went by, that I would be informed when the files were to be shipped from Cambridge and started on their way across the Channel.

I was allotted dormitory space in a dank sort of building, but as I spent a lot of time with the OWI press section I began to meet some interesting people who weren't happy with their accommodations either. Before long I was sharing a flat in Shepherds Market with Hank Foster, a correspondent from *Reader's Digest.*

Shepherds Market was a fascinating jumble of little shops and ancient stores and pubs. Our apartment was on the second floor of one of these, to put it kindly, ramshackle little wooden buildings. The Market was also the official domain of a number of beautifully turned out ladies of the evening, afternoon, or maybe morning. They all had well groomed little dogs on leashes and made the area resemble a stage set just after the curtain had gone up and the audience was waiting for major characters to appear.

One of the ladies had a post in the doorway of the stairs that led up to our apartment. Hank and I always greeted her in a friendly way whenever we met in passing. Her name was Ariadne.

Late one afternoon I walked into the Market after a rough day. Ariadne stood in the doorway looking weary and downcast.

"Tough day," I said.

Ariadne nodded. "I've about had it," she said. "I think I'll call a cab and go home." There is no way that Ariadne's pronunciation of the English language can be written phonetically—except perhaps by Professor Higgins.

"Don't you live around here?"

She looked at me in wonderment. "Course I don't, I wouldn't live in a neighborhood like this." She picked up her little dog and set off in the direction of Berkeley Square.

We Americans were issued British ration cards which we sometimes used ourselves but mostly we did supplementary shopping for British friends. There was a fishmonger in the Market, and one day the word went out that he had a small supply of Dover sole. I joined the queue hoping that there would be some left by the time it was my turn.

A lady one behind me began to talk with a friend of hers a little farther down the queue. The sirens went off and we all dove for some cover. We didn't need it because the bomb landed far over on the dock area. The queue reformed with people in the exact positions they held before the sirens.

The lady one behind turned back to her friend and said, "Mrs. Brown says she doesn't like these new bombs as well as she liked the old ones."

I knew right then that there was no way Britain was going to lose this war.

As a Civil Service employee I had a number indicating my grade, which was established by how much I was getting paid. I've forgotten what my grade was, but I know its corresponding rank in the Army was major. I had bought a class A uniform in New York, but I never wore it in England. When we went up to the warehouse in Cambridge we had to wear Army clothes of some kind and as I remember it the dress code specified Army fatigue jackets and pants, leggings of some sort, and Army boots.

These were the outfits we wore when we boarded the truck to take us up to Cambridge. This was the British version of our Nissen Huts—a cavernous sort of place.

Our plain pine file boxes, looking depressingly like coffins, were organized in groups along one wall. The material we had sorted, coded for filing and packed in cardboard boxes in London came up in the truck with us: thirty copies of each item to be properly filed in the thirty sets of file boxes.

Our warehouse was close to an RAF bomber base, and when we had to stay over, the RAF housing officer always found decent accommodations for us.

Close to the boundaries of the base there was of course a pub, the name of which I shall keep confidential to protect the innocent. My ID papers indicated that I was a "Major (Ass.)" It was a label that caused civilians to laugh and Military Police to glower. The offending abbreviation stood for Assimilated. And it was supposed to protect me, in the event that I was captured by the enemy, from being imprisoned with common soldiers instead of being put in with officers of comparable rank. I never was captured so I don't know whether it would have worked or not.

It was not official, but the pub I went to was the one the officers went to. The enlisted men had a pub of their own. They all liked it that way. The base was home to part of a wing of heavy Lancaster bombers, great four-engined beasts that were used in the night bombing raids on Berlin. Once I saw the whole group take off. It was a tremendous experience, and a sad and harrowing one for I knew that some of the fine young men that I might have been drinking with the night before would not be coming home.

But the pub was always filled with cheer and humor. There was no other way to respond to the demands of the job they were doing. After a few hours I was accepted as a visiting Yank who had at least come a long way to take some part in the effort.

One night the laughter was convulsive. It was a day when the King had come to award medals for various degrees of outstanding service to kingdom and crown. One pilot told me what everybody was laughing so hard about. And again I can't reproduce the way the story was told.

"Well, there was the King coming down the line of the lads that were going to get the George Cross. He'd stop and read the citation; His Majesty, you know, has a bit of a stutter. (I didn't know that.) and he came to a pesky little Welsh gunner and read off something like this: 'that on the thirteenth of Ju-Ju-Ju-July you d-d-d-d-did shoot down a Fu-fu-fu-fu-fu-Focke-fighter from your b-b-b-badly damaged air c-c-c-craft.'

Instead of keeping his bloody mouth shut, the gunner said,

'I'm s-s-s-s-sorry your M-M-M-M-Majesty, it wasn't wu-wu-one F-f-f-f-Focke Wulf it was t-t-t-t-two Fu-fu-fu-Focke Wulfs.'

The King smiled down at the stubby little chap and said, 'I'm s-s-s-sorry, my b-b-boy, there's only one fu-fu-fucking medal.'"

We sang a lot in our pub. "I've Got a Sixpence," "Roll Me Over in the Clover," "The Jolly Tinker," "Bless Them All." The verb "bless" in the last-named ballad was sometimes replaced by a verb that was very rude indeed.

The Yanks in England were a favorite topic of conversation: how they got along and how they didn't. One young Scot told us that he had gotten a letter from his parents complaining about how the Yanks had taken over the town. They were rowdy, his parents said, and not only rowdy but they had a dirty song they liked to sing. A delegation called on the commanding officer to ask that he forbid the singing of that particular song.

At this point the speaker paused and I realized it was a cue for me to ask the proper question. I fell right into the trap.

"What song was that?" I asked.

"One of your best known ones," the Scot said, "called Yank my doodle it's a dandy."

The dialogue brought down the house—as I gathered it had before.

Our units got more comprehensive, but back in London at our weekly meetings I could get no reasonable answer as to why they were not being used. My little group on North Audley Street was getting restive and I didn't blame them. I got permission to make a few trial excursions in England as warm-up exercises. We took units to Manchester and Coventry where I learned one of the saddest secrets of the war. In November 1940 a massive German air raid had struck Coventry causing great damage, including the destruction of the magnificent cathedral, and tragic loss of life. The raid took place within weeks after the British had cracked one of the major German codes. The British Cabinet knew that the raid was going to take place, but could not warn the city because that would have advertised to the Germans that their code had been broken.

The flying bombs continued, and if anything, increased in number. I began to see more and more of people from the British Ministry of Information and volunteered to serve on a couple of projects. One was to help publish a little newspaper that was air dropped over France to inform the French about who and what the Allies were and what they were doing. The paper was produced in the loft of a building off Fleet Street. It was diverting work and gave me a chance to use some of the reference materials that I took from our own files. The compositors and printers worked nights and days beneath a vaulted glass roof, under the circumstances hardly ideal working conditions.

A few times I joined a crew that was studying the effects of bomb blasts. We had a ready room and as soon as one of the V-1's hit, our squad would get to the scene as fast as we could to note and report the damage.

The scene at the bomb sites was always pretty much the same.

The ambulances and fire engines always got there before we did and by the time we located the street there was usually a strange quiet.

Then, one by one, the doors of the undamaged houses would open and in most cases a woman would appear carrying cups of tea on a tray with one hand and a broom with the other. She would set the broom against the side of the door, pass the tea tray around until all the cups were gone, and go back and sweep off the steps of her house.

The German buzz bombing began a week after D-Day, the 6th of June, and lasted until the first week of September when the V-2's started. It was estimated later that the V-1's had killed about 14,000 people.

There was much speculation about how accurate the bombs were. In the old city of London there was an ancient round, domed building that was designated on certain maps as the Royal Arsenal. It hadn't been an arsenal for several hundred years, but it gave the British War Office pause for thought when it was hit right on the top by two V-1's within a period of two weeks. It turned out, after all the German documents from the launching sites had been analyzed, that all the bombs were aimed at the West End's Marble Arch—theoretically the geographical center of London. It was never hit.

The cross-Channel commando raids on the French coast were great morale builders for a people who were tired of taking whatever the enemy was handing out and were eager to do some damage of their own. Consequently the return of commando raiding parties was often covered by BBC radio correspondents waiting on the beach to broadcast an account of the raid.

On one occasion the reporter picked the first man he could grab, put the microphone in the face of his victim and said, "Tell us, what was it like?"

A mincing, effeminate voice went out over the full BBC radio network: "Oh, it was just awful—all that noise and all those people..."

BBC control cut him off the air before he could say another word. The case of the fairy commando was hooted at all over England, but what was broadcast was only part of the story. Colonel Robert Henriques, commando commandant, told the rest months later.

The commando team that had been assigned the mission, lost one of its members in a motorcycle accident an hour before jump-off time. A replacement was quickly assigned from another group. As the landing craft neared the French coast the platoon sergeant gave orders to black-up. While his men went through the usual routine of blackening their faces with a greasy cream, the sergeant kept his eye on the new man. The new team member produced a large gold compact, flipped it open and, studying his face in the mirror, carefully applied black powder with a large pink puff.

The sergeant made a note of this behavior. When the commandos hit the beach they were pinned down instantly by raking fire from German machine gunners concealed in the base of a stone windmill.

The sergeant called for volunteers to deal with the problem so they could get on with their work. No one volunteered. The sergeant pointed to the new man and said, "You go."

Without hesitation the man crawled back into the water and made his way 200 yards down the beach. In a low crouch he moved like a shadow to the wooden door in the side of the windmill. Holding his Sten machine pistol at ready, he kicked open the door.

Down the beach his mates heard his high shrill voice scream, "This is going to kill you...," followed by the murderous pounding of his weapon. The raid was a success, doing much damage.

The man, of course, was the commando who had been cut off the air.

The White Tower restaurant was a popular meeting place for lunch. One day we overheard some Royal Navy officers discussing the qualities of the German military mind. The officers were from one of the British minesweepers which regularly swept up mines that Germans had laid in one area, the day before. The following day the Germans would come back and lay more mines in the same area. One day our friends at the next table stayed home and the following day the Germans came back and blew themselves up on their own mines. When German survivors were rescued they were outraged. Such inefficiency, they sputtered, would never be tolerated in the German Navy.

The days went on. More French cities were liberated. More weekly meetings were held in which the future of the Information

Centers was not even on the agenda and, despite my pleading, was ruled out as an agenda item.

Of all the correspondents I met during that period Bill Johnson of *Time, Inc.* is the only one I have seen on a more or less regular basis ever since. I met him one night at a largish party in favor of some ranking member of the Armed Forces. At parties of this size I always tend to move as far away from the center of the action as I can—after performing my requisite social duties. At this party I saw a man who seemed to be standing as far away from the proceedings as he could without leaving the room. I suspected his mood to be compatible. I introduced myself and in ten minutes we both left to find a bar where we could drink in a more civilized environment. The price of the free drinks at such parties was too high.

Bill was putting up at the Dorchester on what had become known as the correspondents' floor. Hemingway was there, recovering from a severe head injury resulting from an auto accident. Martha Gelhorn, his wife, was on the same floor but they weren't working at their marriage with any consistency. The irrepressible Bob Capa was there too. His name wasn't Capa and nobody called him Bob. He was a great combat photographer who was so alive that being with him was an event in itself.

I finally ended up in a room at the Dorchester myself. The hotel was a big, solid mass of concrete and brick. I don't know about the others but I thought a flying bomb would just dent it. My room was not on the famous floor so I didn't meet Hemingway, or Hemingstein, as many called him, until later in Paris. But Bill told me he was unhappy, drinking heavily and keeping everyone who would listen awake all night as loyal audiences.

A reporter named Mary Welch, a tough young woman with a deceptively soft, heart-shaped face, asked Bill if a room could be found for her at the Dorchester. Bill found one small single room, took that himself and gave Mary and her roommate Connie Ernst his larger room. Later on Mary married Hemingway and Connie married one of the great American publishers of my time, Mike Bessie.

Bill was a great companion. He told me inside stories about odd happenings in the various bureaucracies and committees that normally intelligent people create during wartime. One of these was a committee which held, reasonably, that one of the major causes of wars was children being taught history with a purely national perspective. Textbooks in the postwar world must be much more historically objective. Bill had a friend on the Anglo-American section which was studying each other's history books. The friend told the following story of an incident in one of the committee meetings.

"I was saying that my study of the most popular and widely used British history that young people studied gave a brief and superficial account of the American Revolution and American history since that time.

"My British counterpart said that he thought the whole matter was given due importance and saw no reason for a new version."

Bill's friend wasn't ready to let the point go uncontested—"I said that it was my feeling that the average Englishman knew very little about American history. For instance, I don't think very many Englishmen know that in 1812 the British burned Washington.

"My fellow committee member said that surely that must be an unsubstantiated allegation. I said it wasn't. It was a fact. He shook his head and changed the subject. After the meeting he stopped me in the hall and asked if it was really true that in 1812 the British had burned Washington or was I just pulling his leg.

"I said it was absolutely true. He shook his head sadly and said, 'I knew we burned Joan of Arc but I thought Washington died a natural death.'"

Paris was liberated on August 25th and the members of the Information Center program went on sorting incoming material and keeping the thirty sets of materials up to date. I became so obnoxious about the whole stalled operation that one of my superiors in the London OWI came down to our office one day and told me that unless I quieted down I would be sent back to Washington "with prejudice." All Civil Service folk know this is the most severe punishment that can be meted out in the field.

I said that I would insist on being returned "with prejudice" because I would consider it a permanent disgrace to be associated any longer with this botched-up operation.

He answered rudely. My secretary threw an ashtray at him and he left. It turned out she had been his secretary once.

Shortly after the liberation of Paris, while I was wondering what kind of retribution was being planned for my act of insubordination, I had a strange telephone experience with Bill Johnson.

He was doing an interview with someone ten or twelve miles outside of London and had called me for a little information that I just happened to have. In the middle of a sentence he stopped and said, "What was that?"

"What was what?" I had time to say before I heard an explosion. It sounded like a very large bomb indeed. As a matter of fact it was the first of the more advanced German V-2 rocket bombs.

Many people heard the explosion and were puzzled by the news story in the London papers the next morning concerning the explosion of a marmalade factory outside the city.

You never heard a V-2 coming. In some ways this was a relief and in some ways not. Different people reacted in different ways. The British Government, in private, was horrified to be informed that the first four V-2's marked the corners of an exact square around the city of London. That turned out to be an accident, too.

I didn't have too much time to figure out which bomb I liked better and I don't know what decision Mrs. Brown came to either. A couple of weeks later I got orders that took me out of London. I was glad to go. A few months of going to bed every night wondering whether you were going to wake up in the morning was enough. Even combat troops on leave stayed away from the tortured city.

I was transferred to the OWI Press Section and sent to Paris on a special assignment to work with the liberated French book publishers.

I never did find out what happened to the information collections that our group had worked on with such uncomplaining devotion. The finished files looked a lot like coffins, so for all I know somebody may well have buried them.

However, I finally did find out why the program was aborted. The Army refused to permit civilians under the jurisdiction of the State Department to follow the troops into France. PWD SHAEF (Psychological Warfare Department) would have been glad to have the operation under its control, but my superiors did not want to chance losing the credit for such a sensible program.

Getting to Paris was thrilling. My new assignment was equally exciting. I was back with book publishers again. I had studied French enough so that I felt that with practice I could get along. It was marvelous to be in a great city that was, physically, almost untouched by the war. There had been some desultory fighting within the city, but compared to London it looked almost exactly as I remembered it.

The German occupying forces had treated Paris and its people— except for Jews and members of the resistance—with unusual decency for the most part. As the cultural capital of Western Europe for centuries the Germans had an almost unbelievable neurotic reverence for Paris. Of course they started looting the city systematically as soon as their troops captured it, but that was not only a conqueror's right, it was his duty.

The Paris office of the OWI was close to the Place de l'Opera in a building that looked like a French version of New York's Flatiron building. The Hotel Astra, the OWI billet, was about six blocks away down a side street. It was small, well kept, the food was fine and the downstairs bar was informal and welcoming. And it welcomed a strange assortment of people. Two of my favorites were Fred Lindsay and Sam Foxx. They had been members of the elite 1st Special Service Force which had been formed and trained to drop on Hitler's Berchtesgaden retreat. This plan was abandoned, but they had seen fierce action in Italy and in the invasion of Southern France. Sam was the brother of baseball's famous Jimmy Foxx, and once in a while they played together on the same team. Shot up too badly for more active duty, Fred was running a car company in Paris. This designation meant a military garage where cars of all kinds were serviced and kept in shape for the use of brass—and friends.

Soon after I was installed in the Astra I met the two men who were to be my closest friends for the next year. David Penn was a radio correspondent who was somehow attached to the State Department. I don't think either of the principals knew just what the official attachment was. Steve Campbell was bilingual in French and after a double set of missions with the 9th Airforce was made a military attaché at the Paris embassy. We soon became as inseparable as circumstances permitted.

My job had no description except to make myself useful in whatever ways anybody wanted. The anybodies turned out to be the OWI, SHAEF, and the American Embassy.

At the end of the first week I made an important resolution: I had to organize my duties and my time. At the end of the second week I gave up trying. It was impossible.

The first thing that had happened was that I was put in charge of the paper warehouse in which was stored all the paper that the Allies had sent to Paris for the American and British forces of occupation. Presumably the French had paper of their own—an assumption that was completely unfounded.

The huge rolls of paper, most of which had been unloaded on the Normandy docks, were of varying quality and dimensions. A great many rolls had been soaked in sea water. Many had been handled by giant hooks which almost destroyed their usefulness.

An inventory had to be kept and every withdrawal had to have my signature before the warehouse could release it. The British needed paper for their newspaper, we needed it for *Yank*. Everybody needed paper to run on big presses; to be cut into poster sizes; to be cut in letter sizes; to be cut into memo size. Everybody wanted special paper for special uses.

I was sent out to prepare a list of the operating French printers, what size presses they had and of what printing capacity.

All this required a great deal of getting around Paris. One night at the Astra bar I asked Sammy Foxx if he could promote a jeep for my use. He gave me a Foxxy grin and said I'd have one as soon as he repainted an odd jeep he just happened to have and put on registration numbers that would defy identification. It was a good jeep. I named it The Maus and I loved it. Of course the only way to lock a jeep was to take out the rotor, but as many of us carried a spare rotor it was chancy.

The climax of my paper dealing came as a result of a call from Matt Adams of SHAEF's G2, or intelligence department. He wanted me to find some paper on which they could print their invasion maps of Germany. The paper had to be heavy and coated. We didn't have paper that was either heavy or coated. I was told to go find some. I sought out the printers—big, medium and small. No one had the kind of paper Supreme Headquarters needed.

But one printer took me to a storage area in the rear of his plant and showed me pile after pile of beautifully printed maps on heavy coated paper. I asked him what they were and he told me they were invasion maps of England that he had printed for the Germans.

I picked up one of the maps; oddly enough, it covered the houses and roads of an area of Scotland of which Keith County was part. I turned the map over and held it up to the light to test its opacity. There was no show-through at all. I had found my paper.

Supreme Headquarters wasn't ecstatic, but there wasn't any alternative. Matt ordered the invasion maps of Germany printed on the reverse side of the German invasion maps of England. I naturally kept one which I planned to have framed with glass on both sides as a showpiece of the nature of war, but somehow it got lost.

One of the pieces of information I had for the French publishers was that one branch of the American government had gone to considerable trouble and expense to have new translations made of American classics to go on sale in France as soon as things had settled down. I believe there were thirty titles ranging from the *Federalist* through Emerson, Hawthorne, Melville, Lewis, Faulkner, Steinbeck and Hemingway. These were sturdily bound paperback volumes that were destined to go on the market at fifteen francs. There were, I think, editions of 10,000 copies of each title.

I never discovered whose plan this was and what it was supposed to accomplish, but French publishers were far from pleased. They called on me in my office and very politely asked why we hadn't sent them the paper and let them print the books.

I had no answer for that. When they asked what the retail price was going to be and I told them, they lost most of their politeness. When they started putting books on the market again, similar books would have to be priced at 300 francs. What were we trying to do, the eminent French publisher Gaston Gallimard wanted to know, make them look like the worst kind of profiteers?

I had no answer for that either but promised to refer their attitudes to Washington. As it turned out I didn't have to. My favorite mentor, Harold Guinzburg, showed up to see how things were going. We sat in the Astra bar talking over what could be done. While we couldn't stop the books' arrival—they were in the middle of the Atlantic—we could reprice them to 300 francs when they got here and defuse some of the French publishing reaction.

Harold got an okay for this action from Washington and I approached the French publishers with this solution.

It was fine, they said, but the new price would mean that the United States Government would be making a large profit on the operation. In all good conscience, they said, they could not permit this money to leave France. So we were faced with a brand new problem. I asked for advice from Washington and didn't get any.

Then Harold appeared in Paris again and he and I had another meeting in the Astra bar. This time we made a plan that we were confident would be a creative solution to the problem.

We approached the French Academy and said that we would shortly have a significant number of francs at our disposal, and wouldn't it be a good idea to have the Academy and a suitable institution in the United States use the funds for postwar student exchange programs?

The American Embassy in Paris thought it was a great idea. The French publishers, after due consideration, agreed that it satisfied their concept of fiscal propriety. Gil Winant, the American Ambassador to the Court of St. James, said it was the best idea the OWI ever had.

The OWI people in Washington said they would have to refer the plan to the proper Congressional committee. By the time we got the decision in Paris it was November, 1944. The answer was no. A government agency was not allowed to indulge in a profit-making enterprise. I never did find out what happened to the books.

About the same time that the decision got to us we heard that Cass Canfield had been posted to Paris to take charge of the OWI operation in France and North Africa. It was wonderful news in more ways than one.

Cass was a distinguished publisher and a ranking member of the Board of Economic Warfare. Protocol would demand that the French publishers could talk to no one but him. This left me with nothing to do except the basic OWI job of "improving relations with the French, of keeping them informed concerning the United States, of getting information about our war effort into their press, radio and in books." The words are Cass' in his fine book *Up & Down & Around*.

When Cass came to Paris from North Africa he brought several members of his staff with him. One female propaganda expert told us about a social change that the war had brought to Tunisia. Before the war when a Sheikh took his household on an outing his wives walked behind him at a respectful distance. The defeat of Rommel's Afrika Corps permitted the resumption of these pleasant excursions, but now, considering the number of German and Allied land mines still unaccounted for, the wives led the way followed at a prudent distance by their lord and master.

I still had the paper warehouse to keep track of, but by this time M. Robert Blanchard—who owned the place—knew what the rules were and had proven his honesty. We did a lot of our business on the telephone. About this time an attractive, middle-aged man was moved, with a small desk, into my office. I was never told what his job was. So I figured it was none of my business. In about a month he moved out. Ten years later I ran into him on Park Avenue outside the Racquet Club. I asked him what his assignment had been and what it had to do with me.

"Somebody assumed that you must be black marketing some of the paper from your warehouse," he said.

"I considered it, but I'm too careless to be a good crook. I decided not to."

"It took me a month to find out you weren't. Don't you want to know who sent me?"

I said I didn't.

There was a predatory black market going, however. Of course the most wanted product was American cigarettes. The French had cruel laws to impose on people who got caught at it.

Under circumstances I never understood, eight American GI's were tried and found guilty of dealing in black-market cigarettes. After sentences had been passed out, Camus, whose famous underground newspaper *Combat* was now above ground, wrote a front-page editorial for his paper. After setting the scene it read as follows: (The names, of course, are fictitious.)

Allen, H.W., Specialist (E6), Harrington, Minn.   15 years.

Bronson, J.M., Pvt. 1st class, East River, VT.   20 years.

Colson, J.P. Pvt. 1st class, Meadowbrook, Ill.   15 years.

Eddy, M.C., Corporal, Northumberland, NY.   20 years.

Manning, C.J., Corporal, Santa Clara, Ariz.   15 years.

Polemski, R., Pvt., Mountainside, W.Va.   15 years.

Rosen, B., Corporal, Mount Holly, Va.   20 years.

Sand, R.L., Sergeant, Lake Marcy, Louis.   20 years.

The editorial ended with the lines:

"These young Americans traveled thousands of miles to offer their lives for the freedom of France. Frenchman, that American cigarette you are smoking. How does it taste?"

First there was no paper, then winter brought a scarcity of coal. The French got almost none. In the OWI office the teletype operator, a good man named Earl Morgan, used to wear mittens when he wasn't pounding his keys. Otherwise a lot of time would be lost. When his mittens weren't enough to keep his fingers flexible he hammered away on a typewriter the Germans had left behind. Of course Earl didn't know any German so he just typed word-length collections of letters. At one time he had a stack of a couple of hundred sheets. In an uninspired moment I packed them up and sent them down to SHAEF to an officer friend, Matt Adams, for analysis. Weeks later I regretted the act. Matt was not pleased. He said I had caused one cryptographer a nervous breakdown.

American Army food was still the best in Paris and our meals at the Hotel Astra were fine. As often as seemed reasonable I invited members of the French press for meals. Charles Gombaud, from the French picture magazine *Match,* came several times. One special day our table had a bowl of fruit on it. Fresh fruit had been unknown in Paris for four years. When we had finished our lunch and our talk I asked Charles if he would like to take a piece of fruit with him. He chose an orange and we walked out to the street together.

A young French mother holding her small son by the hand pointed to the orange in Charles's hand. She bent down and said,

"Ca c'est un orange." The child, of course had never seen one.

Charles stopped, turned around, and put the orange in the little boy's hand.

The mother looked unbelievingly at Charles then turned to her son again. "Et ca c'est un miracle."

I loved the French people. The ones I got to know were tough-minded realists who had a quarrelsome love affair with each other and the world. They didn't like soldiers much. Not even their own. Their farmlands had been fought over by too many soldiers from too many countries for too many years.

One story the OWI Press Section picked up was of particular delight to me. Someone had thought up the idea of giving GI mine detectors to French farmers along the shores of the invasion beaches, which had been pretty solidly mined by the Germans as they retreated. A delegation with the mine detectors went down to the coast and distributed them, along with instructions for their use. There had been a few instances of farmers being wounded or killed. As soon as the farmers found out the detectors were both free and harmless they accepted them. All except one.

He said he had no need for one because there were no mines on his farm. When asked what made him so sure about this he said that after the St. Lo break-out of the Allied forces there had been a compound nearby in which German prisoners were kept until sent to more permanent quarters. He had asked the American major who was in charge of the compound for a favor. The major said sure. What did he want?

What the farmer asked for, and got, was a detachment of German prisoners to do a full, goose-stepping close-order drill all over his whole farm. The Major said he was happy to oblige.

"Were there any mines?" we asked.

"Not then and not now," the farmer replied.

More OWI personnel arrived every day, and they all knew more about how to do what was officially designed to be done than I did. My experiences in London had taught me, among other things, that I was not suited to Civil Service. The Paris publishing scene wouldn't need me after Cass got here. Harold Guinzburg had resigned (for the third and last time) from the OWI. I needed a plan, and I had a half-formed one in my mind.

Newspapers and magazines had been full of dramatic news pictures of the war, some taken by Signal Corps photographers and some by combat photographers like Capa. My idea was to create a documentary photo record of a soldier's day. How he slept, how he ate, how he did all the jobs that had to be done. How he fought and how he died.

As far as I knew no such book existed or was being planned. I cabled Holt and asked them to send me some reviews that said I knew how to put a picture book together.

When the affidavits came I organized a presentation of my project and, because I knew only one man at SHAEF, sent it along to Matt Adams. In a surprisingly short time he called and said he had pushed it along to the proper channels and I would be hearing from somebody sometime.

"It may take a while," he said. "I'm not so sure anybody is as eager to get you out of Paris as I am."

"Are you referring to the German manuscript I sent you?"

"I am indeed," he said. "The sooner I get you in a combat zone the better I'll sleep."

I settled down to wait. I released batches of paper to French magazines so they could publish issues that had a few nice things to say about our war effort. One magazine published an entire issue about a French town that had been adopted by an American town. It was full of pictures illustrating how much good the relationship had done.

One day I was invited, or summoned, to the Embassy and told there was an errand for me to perform. Charles Scribner, Hemingway's publisher, had sent over in the diplomatic pouch a contract that needed Mr. Hemingway's signature. Would I be good enough to find Mr. Hemingway, have him sign the contract and return the document to them? They thought he was somewhere in Paris.

Thought? Everyone knew he was in Paris and everyone knew he was at the Ritz. So I went over.

The big man opened the door, smiled and asked me in. He was alone. At that time I didn't know how extraordinary that was. I told him who I was and why I had come. He said he thought we should have a drink and he'd sign whatever it was later on.

We drank and talked the rest of the afternoon. I found him easy, gracious, with none of the fierce projection of his toughness that I had heard so much about. He soon found out that I was both a writer and a publisher and accepted me with no disparagement.

Later I found out that J.D. Salinger had had the same impression after a one-on-one visit with Hemingway.

Hemingway told me a long story about his court martial—which turned out not to have been a court martial at all—what the charges were and how he had answered them. I had heard at least seven different accounts of the actions that had caused the so-called court martial, and was delighted to listen to the account given by the central figure.

It all had to do with what went on at Rambouillet, a town about 30 kilometers outside Paris, on the days of August 19-20. The cast of the drama varied depending on who was telling the story. One version has it that Marty Gelhorn, his present wife, and Mary Welch, his future wife, were both there. E.H. didn't mention this. Almost all the sources agree that E.H. was in effective command of ten or thirty French guerilla fighters who were kept busy patrolling the area and fending off vastly superior German forces, including two, four, or a dozen German Tiger tanks.

All accounts have him dressed in full combat gear with grenades and sidearms and no correspondent's identification, and living in a room piled with German Teller mines that had been dug up by his "army."

Another version has it that the mines were American and had been removed by E.H.'s partisan irregulars to permit the passage of Allied vehicles. I first heard the Rambouillet story from Sam Boal, a close friend of Hemingway's and Sam's was different from anybody else's. He had it that Hemingway had all the mines resown on the approach through Rambouillet that General LeClerc had picked for his armored division to use on its triumphal entry into Paris, and (the advance) had been held up for hours while the mines were removed. The more stories about the whole affair I heard, including Hemingway's own, the more it sounded like the famous blindfolded men describing the elephant.

While we were talking, E.H. took several phone calls and after one said he had to leave, but asked me to come back the next day at the same time and he'd sign the paper.

I came away impressed. He had spoken affectionately and admiringly of many people and had belittled no one.

The next morning Matt Adams called to tell me that my project had been approved and I would be getting orders to report to the headquarters of the Tenth Infantry Regiment.

"It's a regiment of the 5th Division," Matt said. "Where are they?"

"The 5th is part of Patton's Third Army," Matt paused, "and we're never quite sure where all the elements of it are, but by the time your orders are cut we'll know where to send you."

E.H. was alone again when I got to the Ritz that afternoon. When I told him about my new assignment he grew very enthusiastic about it. He asked me whether this was my first trip up to the line and I told him it was.

He began to walk around and around the room giving me all kinds of advice on how to avoid being killed, what to wear, how to tell a good officer from a bad one, and always, when there was food to be had, to eat all I could because I'd never know when I was going to eat again. He said I was luckier than most correspondents because I wouldn't have to leave the advance combat zone to find some way to file a story. I could stick with the men who were doing the real work.

He asked me about my boyhood—particularly as it was associated with guns. I told him that I had shot woodchucks with a .22 and a Winchester .30-.30 carbine. I was not a hunter. He inquired if I had had any military training, and I confessed to six weeks in a Citizens Military Training Camp program back in the 30's somewhere.

The official rifle of the Army then—at least the part of the Army I was in at Fort Ethan Allen—was the 1903 bolt- action Springfield. The first time I fired my piece on the range the bolt blew out backward just ticking my ear. After that I had little confidence in the weapon.

E.H told me some stories about his boyhood—most of which I had read—but it was fine to listen and watch him telling them. We had a good time and he asked me to call him after I got my orders and knew exactly where I was going.

My orders hadn't come through by the first week of December. By this time E.H. had been through the hell of the Hurtgen Forest. When he got back to Paris he, I was told, had had enough of the war and was looking for a return flight to the USA.

I did spend most of one afternoon with him, though. He was sick and tired—not despondent, just bone tired. We talked about how the wild boars had been driven out of the Forest by the fighting and now were being hunted on the outskirts of Paris.

Several times he went to his closet and took out the big white sheepskin coat that he called his Kraut jacket.

"You're going to need something like this, maybe I'll give you this one." Then he'd hang the coat back in the closet. During one of these closet openings I saw a neat stack of well-wrapped packages. The top of one was torn open and what I saw looked like one of the beautiful French thousand-franc notes.

I asked him what the packages were. He laughed and said that two GI's from the 4th Division (E.H.'s favorite) had gotten their first ten-day leave since D-Day and set out for Paris. On the way they had knocked off a German paymaster's vehicle loaded with what they thought was colorful French propaganda of some kind. They were used to getting paid in U.S. invasion currency—dollar-bill size notes—so they knew what money looked like, or thought they did. But they tossed a dozen or so packages of the pretty paper into their jeep and used it to make fires to warm up their food on the trip. But then they had run out of real money and as a joke offered a piece of the propaganda at some bistro.

E.H. laughed and said, "They said it acted just like real money and used all they could before they had to rejoin their unit. This is what they had left over. They thought I'd like to have some."

"What are you going to do with it?"

"Keep it until I leave," E.H. said. "Maybe they'll come back for it." He reached for the big winter coat again, then shrugged his shoulders and said he guessed he might need it again and shut the closed door.

And he certainly did. On December 17th the Germans launched a huge counter-attack along an eighty-mile front in the Ardennes in what became known as the Battle of the Bulge. E.H. was down with chills, fever and constant vomiting.

In a matter of hours he bundled himself up in two fleece-lined coats—one of them almost mine—and was on his way to join the men of his beloved 4th division which had taken the first German blow.

I didn't see him again until late 1946 when Sam Boal and I joined a lunch group at Toots Shor's. E.H. was at his loudest and most arrogant. His New York circle was eating it up and after a while Sam and I left.

I'll always remember the quiet hours with him in Paris as I will always reread and be inspired by the best of his writing.

Christmas was a sad and lonely time for all of us, but we couldn't help comparing it to the grim holiday which gave the French so little to celebrate and less to celebrate it with.

Early in January I was alerted to the arrival of a group of writers and magazine publishers from the States and requested to cooperate with their needs. I was delighted to learn that the group would include two of my favorite people—Stanley Young and his wife Nancy Wilson Ross. I won't identify the others on this junket because they had an assortment of outrageous requests. For example, one VIP magazine publisher wanted me to find a French family which:

1) Had lost the husband in a heroic battle with the Germans,
2) Had a daughter who had been raped, preferably more than once, by brutal German soldiers,
3) Had a noble son who was blowing up bridges with his comrades, in the French underground, and
4) Had an indomitable wife who was the key link in the rescue network for downed Allied airmen.

I said that I would do my best to find such a family, and in the meantime there were a couple of things I'd like them to see. I led them to the rear of one of the buildings that had become an American officers' mess. Long lines of French men and women stretched away from a dozen or so roll- off containers.

A visiting editor asked what they were waiting for. I explained that they were waiting for the containers to be filled with garbage from the noon meal. I added that the lines were longer after dinner.

Next I led our little cavalcade a few blocks down the Avenue de la Grande Armé. A good many well-dressed people lined the curbs. This time, before anyone had time to ask what the people were waiting for, a coal truck came bumping up the cobbled street. Every time it bumped pieces of coal dropped from the load and people darted out with pans to pick up whatever they could.

I thought to cheer up our little group by telling them one of the most quoted of the French anecdotes of the occupation. This story, was referred to as "The German Officer and the Occupied French Girl."

With rare restraint, the story began with the German officer getting out of bed, dressing and going to the door. He clicked his heels and said, "In nine months you will have a baby. You have my permission to call him Otto."

As he opened the door the French girl called over, "In eight days you will have a rash. You have my permission to call it measles."

When they left for Le Bourget to return home, Nancy and Stanley said that the group had not voted me its most popular guide.

On the 13th and 14th days of February the combined air forces of the United States and Great Britain performed one of the most depraved acts of war in history. On these two days 2,700 Allied bombers destroyed 75 percent of the ancient city of Dresden.

Dresden was a target without either military or strategic importance. It was rumored to have a synthetic fuel laboratory somewhere nearby. This was no more than a rumor. But it was known that the city harbored some 20,000 Allied prisoners.

On the first day 650,000 incendiary bombs were dropped, causing a firestorm. The following day, as rescue and salvage workers poured in from central Germany, the bombing was renewed. No accurate death count was ever established, but all estimates were over 200,000.

None of these figures were available until after the war and no reasonable justification has ever been offered.

In his memoirs Churchill wrote, in passing, that Dresden was "a centre of communications."

Matt Adams finally called on February 19th to tell me that my orders had been cut and I was to present myself at SHAEF headquarters for final briefing and departure.

It sounded like a ceremony but it wasn't. Matt gave me a

two-inch stack of mimeographed sheets that gave my name, serial number, rank (Major Ass.), and confirmed that I was attached to the Tenth Infantry Regiment to "carry out the orders of the Supreme Commander."

"Is that all?"

Matt asked me what more I wanted. I said that I'd have trouble explaining why I was running around imitating a soldier. Matt said that with those orders I wouldn't have to. He gave me a stack of maps of Eastern France and Western Germany. I asked him where I was going. He went on to tell me that they had selected a newspaper photographer, Captain Smith (not his name), to work on the project with me. Captain Smith was on his way over from Flushing, New York where he had been attached to an Army film unit.

"Go to Ettelbruch and ask where the Tenth is. You'll find it."

That was all there was to my final briefing. When I got back to my jeep there was a disconsolate looking private sitting at the wheel. I asked him why and he said that since I was field grade officer I wasn't permitted to drive a jeep. I had to have a driver and he had been assigned to the job. He asked where we were going. When I told him he looked still more disconsolate.

"You don't much want to go back to the line," I said. He said his unit had been almost wiped out in the Ardennes; he had been in a replacement depot ever since and didn't much care where he went as long as it wasn't the line.

I said that I wasn't too keen on having a driver anyway. He suggested that he drive me around the corner out of sight and get out. I thought that was fine. I never even found out what his name was.

It should be reported now that I didn't get the material for the book I wanted. The pictures I wanted were all there to be taken, but there was never a photographer at hand at exactly the right instant. I found the Tenth Infantry without too much trouble. Matt Adams had been right. My orders made it unnecessary to explain anything.

Captain Smith arrived on the scene wearing a class A uniform and carrying a Valpak suitcase. He had his own ideas as to what kind of pictures he was going to take. He spent the first week looking for a puppy because he had set his heart on taking a picture of heroic GI's returning from a patrol, one of whom would be carrying a puppy in his open shirt. He was sure that this picture would make the front page of many newspapers.

He liked his uniform with its captain's bars and he liked being saluted. Nobody liked him. Every time he'd try to take a picture I wanted, the GI's would practice making like Stan Laurel, Oliver Hardy or one of the Three Stooges.

We didn't have to put up with him for very long, though. We had settled in for the night outside a small German town. The Captain and I were bedding down close to an ex-German U-shaped sentry trench when a machine gun opened up on our platoon. I jumped gratefully into the trench, but the Captain sat down on the edge and prepared to slide down on his butt. He hadn't observed that the trench was lined with small fir trees some of which had sharp points.

One of our corpsmen did some quick repair on his injury and sent him back to the regimental aid station. I never saw him again, but years later I was at a party and the subject of the war came up—as it always did—and I was talking about photographers I had known and someone asked if I had run across a certain Captain Smith. I said I had. I was then asked if I knew exactly how he had gotten his saber wound. I said I didn't.

I spent most of the weeks with Company C of the Third Battalion of the Tenth Infantry, crossed the Kyll River and the Rhine with them and over the Main River and into Frankfurt.

This is no place for details of my experiences as a "working soldier," but a few comments may be necessary for clarification.

The first day we moved out, the platoon sergeant pointed to the patch I was wearing on my left shoulder. It was a large white triangle with a big blue US in the center.

"It means I'm a civilian and you shouldn't shoot me," I explained.

"Tear it off," the sergeant said, "it's been sniper bait since Normandy." He asked me if I was armed.

"Of course not. I'm a civilian correspondent and it's against the Geneva Convention for me to be armed."

"Fuck the Geneva Convention. See me during the next break."

When the column stopped he came back with a dozen grenades and a .45 automatic. He asked me if I had ever thrown a grenade. I hadn't. Ten minutes later I had learned how to pull the ring, count, and throw. Same thing with the .45. At the end of the short lesson with the .45 the sergeant said,

"If you're ever in a spot where you think you really need this, don't fire it, throw it." He left the .45 and six grenades with me and said to keep them in the jeep.

Ernie Pyle wrote so well about the men I was with that I won't even try. When we were really in combat I rode with Blackie O'Connor in the .50 caliber jeep. The .50 was mounted on a turret with a 360-degree traverse. It was designated as an anti-aircraft weapon. Blackie explained that this was necessary because the Geneva Convention forbade foot soldiers to shoot each other with anything larger than a .30 caliber weapon. I got to be very fond of Blackie. Once I got my head in the way of the barrel of the .50 as it swung around. It knocked my helmet off and nicked my cheekbone. A tiny trickle of blood appeared. Blackie immediately said he was going to get me a Purple Heart.

"You wounded me," I said, "and you're no enemy."

Blackie claimed it was his reaction to enemy action that caused my wound. I said I was a civilian and wasn't eligible, and I wouldn't accept one even if I were.

In fire fights like the one outside Schwanheim, a suburb of Frankfurt, I ran mortar ammunition in my own jeep and during one lull a pair of clean socks to a GI with a problem.

It's hard to remember details of how you lived during those days. I remember heating shaving water in my helmet with the waxy box K rations came in. I got a haircut sitting on the tread of a light tank. The gunner was a barber who kept his scissors and comb with him. I remember our entire company delaying their Rhine crossing while two medics delivered a baby to a German mother in a nearby town. I remember squad leaders and platoon sergeants making sure their men's foxholes were deep enough and that they slept with enough cover and with loosened boots. These were the kinds of pictures I didn't get.

I remember going for days without changing clothes and looking forward to C rations instead of K, and how good, when we got one, a hot meal tasted. I remember lying in a ditch under machine gun fire with my pants wet with more than ditch water. I knew we would have to move out any minute and I thought, "I can't do it." The ending of Harry Brown's fine novel *A Walk In The Sun* came into my mind. His soldiers were safe behind a stone wall, but one by one they had to get up and sprint toward the farmhouse at the machine gun. The last man waited, knowing that his legs wouldn't work when it was his turn. He was thinking, just as I was, that he couldn't do it. But he did, and his inside voice said, "See, you can do it too." And that was just the way it happened to me.

Later on I found out that Harry Brown was a soldier-poet who had never been anywhere near combat. How did he know?

Somehow the 5th Division had convinced itself that its objective was the capture of Frankfurt, and after that had been accomplished on March 30, its job was done. When the battle for Frankfurt was over our men went on a two-day binge that, judging from the reports I got, was as dangerous as combat.

I said good-bye to my unit and started back for Paris following a route that would take me to Signal Corps film processing facilities so I could try to find the pictures that some of the photographers had taken. Over and over again I was told to go back to the central facility in Paris where I would no doubt find everything in order.

Of course I didn't. My project had a code number, but that couldn't be located. One excellent professional newspaper photographer who had been assigned to me for a week or so presumably had his pictures, but I couldn't find him either.

I was not all that depressed. The failure of the project was mine because I had not realized that no one but a master photographer who was also a soldier could have done the book I had visualized. It was a strange way to get another publishing lesson.

Everyone in Paris was a lot more relaxed than when I had left in February. The weather was fine and spirits were high and exultant. Until April 12th, when FDR died.

The loss was intensified by the idea that Harry Truman was now President of the United States and Commander-in-Chief of its armed forces. Harry Truman? The failed haberdasher from Kansas City? Sure, his Senate committee had done some good work, but who was he? We soon found out.

But the war was clearly almost over; the Allies had won and FDR had died knowing that his country had kept faith with its commitments to the free world.

I had checked in with SHAEF and the OWI and was put back to work. Strange new assignments were dropped in my lap—I didn't have a desk. The strangest one of all became known as the affair of the Millionth Prisoner.

The American Air Force had been evacuating French refugees from Germany in ever-increasing numbers since early May. The OWI thought it would enhance our prestige in France to stage an event that would bring our warm, generous cooperation to the attention of the French nation. After consideration at the highest level the plan was agreed upon.

An attractive young Frenchman—recently freed from a German prisoner of war camp—would be flown into Paris, there greeted by allied generals with great pomp and ceremony and motorcaded away to the obligatory welcome home banquet complete with wife and family.

This was the way it was laid out. All I had to do was to see that it was implemented. For logistical help I was referred to a Colonel Bill Forman, who turned out to be a quiet New Englander with a perpetual half-smile on his angular face. After I had introduced myself and explained my errand I asked him how many prisoners had so far been returned to their homes.

He consulted his records, "One million, forty-six thousand," he said, "do you want me to send some back?"

This established an easy working relationship. Colonel Forman couldn't have been more helpful or accommodating. He told me that the plan was to have the plane carrying our prisoner taxi to the Paris end of the Le Bourget airport building. He would then be escorted to four Allied generals who would greet him while their national anthems were being played. After that he would be whisked away in an open limousine to join a cavalcade of diplomats, politicians and a few retired field marshals. The destination of the motorcade was a sumptuous dining hall on the Place des Vosges where he and his wife and family would be guests of honor of the Republic of France.

The whole thing didn't seem to offer any impossibilities. I asked the Colonel for advice on selecting a prisoner. He walked over to a map on his wall, studied the doodles on it and said that I'd probably have the best luck going up to Lüneburg.

"Lots of prisoners waiting there."

I explained that my friend Larry from the OWI Press Section would be responsible for tracking down the right prisoner.

"Better get him right up there," the Colonel said, "you've only got a week."

I didn't have to worry about the motorcade, or getting the generals, but I did have a few minor responsibilities beyond producing the right prisoner at the right time. I had to find a band that was available and could play the American, French, British and Russian national anthems. I asked the Colonel where I might look for such a group and he said he had no idea.

Neither did the embassies of any of the countries involved. Nor did any branch of anybody's armed forces have any bands that were available for such duty. On the third day I didn't have a prisoner or a band. All I had was a growing desperation.

Finally on the morning of the fourth day a friend at the British Embassy called to say that he had heard of a small group of musicians attached to a regiment of Welsh Guards who happened to be in Paris on some inexplicable errand. He told me how to get in touch with the leader.

That night Larry called from Lüneburg. "I've got the ideal man," he cheered. "He looks like Jean Gabin, he has a wife and two daughters in Paris already, he has won the Croix de Guere and he even speaks English."

"That sounds great. You don't know what a load off my mind that is." I took a deep breath.

"There's just one thing," Larry said.

I waited.

"He doesn't want to come home."

"Well, why the hell not?"

"He's got a good job here with a German general, he's shacked up with a fraulein, he says he never liked his wife and daughters anyway and he's going to stay right where he is. Maybe I should begin looking for another man."

"We haven't got time," I screamed, "you've got to find a French officer to tell him he has to go through with this trip or he'll be shot, or something. It is his sacred duty to France."

Larry said he'd call back the next day. I got up early and told the story to Colonel Bill who said, "That's terrible, just think what would happen if your prisoner escaped." Then he grinned and said he'd get on the phone and see what he could do. I went to find the Welsh Guards band. I found them practicing in the courtyard of a Left Bank hotel. They played well, if a little plaintively.

I told the leader he had a chance to strike a blow for postwar harmony by becoming a part of our celebration. He listened silently, consulted his engagement book and said he thought they could fit it in. They had the necessary music except for the Russian national anthem. He said I would have to supply that. We agreed on the rest of the details. The American general would be first and the band was to play "The Star Spangled Banner." The next general would be French so it would be the "Marseillaise." Following "God Save the King" for the next general would come whatever the Russian national anthem turned out to be. Everything was all set, or it would be if I could supply the right Russian score.

I tried the Russian embassy and got nowhere. I thought for a while I might be detained for interrogation.

Then I went to a French music store where a clerk with a pince-nez and a silly smile told me there were two official Russian national anthems and which one did I want. I told him I wanted the most recently official and carried the score back to the Welsh Guards.

On the fifth day Larry said the prisoner had had a change of heart and decided to come to Paris after all— provided he could bring a friend. After having been reassured that the friend was not the fraulein, I agreed. Now it appeared that if our prisoner changed his mind again we had a backup.

Most of the sixth day I spent making sure that everyone knew where they were supposed to be and that a space had been cleared for the Welsh Guards band close enough to the greeting locations so they could be heard. Larry called early on the seventh day to say that all was well, but the prisoner was growing more and more restive as the hours passed. The plane was due to land at Le Bourget at 2 p.m. sharp.

By 1 p.m. I had my generals in a row about twenty feet apart. First was our man, General Kingman, and then a magnificently uniformed French general almost as tall as de Gaulle. The British general was a solid, short man with a no-nonsense expression. The Russian general looked both fierce and unhappy. He was fourth in line.

We stood at ease, eyeing our wristwatches and listening for the well-known sound of a C-47. The Welsh musicians were playing what may well have been their own national anthem.

Then, suddenly, a French officer appeared in front of me, saluted, and said he had been informed that I was in charge of these festivities.

I admitted it.

He announced that I had both the flags and the generals in the wrong order. This affair was taking place on the soil of France and therefore the flag of France had to be in the first position.

I answered respectfully—and accurately—that this was in fact Allied soil. It had not yet been returned to the Republic of France.

The French officer saluted me with a look and turned to our General Kingman. After a while General Kingman walked over to where I was standing.

"Don't you think you'd better change the order of the flags?" he said pleasantly enough.

I said I didn't think so at all. The soil was Allied, American planes had brought in all the prisoners and when you asked an American to run an Allied ceremony, whose flag did anyone think he was going to put first?

The General regarded me kindly, "In spite of that uniform you are a civilian, aren't you?"

I said I was.

"In that case," said the General, "I can't very well give you an order, can I?"

"I guess not, General."

The French officer who had been monitoring the conversation turned to me and asked if there was anyone here who could give me an order.

"Lots," I said, pointing to the group of Embassy people gathered twenty yards behind the line of generals. He took off and faced them, his long arms motioning articulately in the air.

A few moments later I was instructed to put the French flag first. I did so and General Kingman, his aide and his flag took up the second position. Somehow with all this moving around the Russian general had moved himself and his hammer and sickle into the third spot. The British general, now in the fourth spot, accepted the new order with grim restraint.

We had just settled down to our waiting when the plane came in. It landed and taxied up to Le Bourget's center entrance—not the one where the reception committee was assembled.

The main doors burst open and a few hundred people attacked

the plane and dragged the prisoner down to the tarmac where an unauthorized French band immediately struck up the "Marseillaise."

Taking advantage of the obligatory immobility of all the French, a couple of General Kingman's aides hauled our prisoner, gently but firmly, down to where our generals were waiting.

When the prisoner was standing at attention, his hand still frozen in salute, I waved my handkerchief in a prearranged signal to the leader of the Welsh band who, not having noticed the change of order in the arrangement of the flags and generals, burst into the strains of "The Star Spangled Banner." Visibly shaken, the French general saluted, clapped the fellow on the back and stepped back without kissing him.

General Kingman did his greeting to the inspiring "Marseillaise" with a warm smile and a handshake.

The opening chords of "God Save the King" caught the Russian general in a rigid salute directed to the prisoner standing in front of him. He dropped his hand, raised it in what was clearly not going to be a salute, then let it fall limply to his side. His eyes were not focused on the prisoner, but on something very far away. Possibly Siberia.

By this time, knowing perfectly well what was coming, the British general's face was set in an expression of bleak acceptance which did not change as the Welshmen wrestled with the strange cadences of the most recently official Russian national anthem.

Then a blessed group of strangely uniformed Frenchmen pounced on the prisoner and installed him in a gleaming open touring sedan. The sirens and trumpets sounded and the affair was over.

Steve and David supported me on our way to the nearest bistro and cauterized my wounds with alcohol.

One French newsman followed our prisoner's friend, the unofficial million and first prisoner, and reported that the refugee was packed into a truck with other refugees and taken to the city for a thorough delousing.

A few weeks after the official end of hostilities in Europe Arthur Brentano, Jr., of the famous bookselling clan, arrived in Paris to see how his beautiful store had survived the conflict. He asked me to come with him to be a qualified witness to the destruction. To Arthur's surprise his key opened the main door. The electricity had not been turned on, but even in the dim light from the unwashed windows it was apparent that everything was in order—except for dust.

The shelves still contained a wide selection of titles but, as Arthur pointed out, a lot more German authors than ever before. He led the way to the manager's office. After inspecting the files and drawers Arthur said it was much neater than his manager had kept things.

He located the checkbook with no trouble and found that there was a credit balance of a large number of francs still in the account. A telephone call to the bank confirmed the amount to the last centime. Arthur clapped his hands in approval and said he'd have the store open in two weeks.

Somehow the incident made me decide to go home as soon as I could. I made out all the required documents of request and waited.

A month later I was still waiting. There had been small jobs for me to do. I could hardly believe that the future of postwar Europe depended on my presence, but I was, justly enough, far down on the list of people who wanted, and deserved, to get home before me.

Finally, sometime after the middle of July, I was sent down to

Camp Lucky Strike—one of the departure camps in the hills above Le Havre. There the act of waiting for an actual berth on a real ship was raised to an art. The most common occupation was painting verbal pictures of what we were going to do after we'd gotten home.

Mostly they were pretty traditional images of home, mother, apple pie, wives, children and well-paid jobs at the end of long vacations.

One West Virginia lad said he was going to sit on the front porch of his cabin in a rocking chair and rock—with the grain.

A West Coast GI said he was going to find a place to live on the edge of a cliff looking out over the Pacific Ocean. Outside his house there was to be a three-sided privy with the open side facing Hawaii. I ran into some men from the 10th Infantry, but none from my battalion. And the weeks passed.

Abruptly one morning our group was ordered to pack up and be ready to leave in an hour. We were ready in fifteen minutes, boarded the bus and began to wait.

We finally made it to the harbor, to the dock, to the gangplank of the S.S. Noordam and to our bunks. It was a calm and pleasant ride home. We walked the decks in a haze of gratitude. I thought of Emily and our boys and how great it would be to be home again. I had cabled Emily with an approximate date of arrival, and when I got to the Gramercy Park Hotel she was at the front desk checking out because I was days overdue. The next day we went to Vermont to join our sons and their grandparents.

After a few days in Vermont I went back to New York to spend some time with my friends at Henry Holt. Everything was fine and it was exciting to be with them again. Bill had hired a sales manager to do my job while I was away and the young man was so good that there was no question of letting him go. The solution was to make me executive editor— whatever that meant—to handle book projects, do promotion and generally work in where I was most effective.

Of course, my immediate family were back to not having a roof of their own over their heads. Bill Sloane lived on South Mountain Road in Rockland County's New City. He had lined up some house rentals for us under the assumption that we would like to come out there to live. We had visited at his home and loved the area.

I took the train from New York to go back up to Vermont to discuss the whole thing with Emily, and ran into one of the most moving "author" experiences any writer ever had.

For some reason I was still wearing a makeshift Army outfit, and when I went down to shave in the Pullman's washroom in the morning I got into conversation with an elderly gent having a pre-breakfast pipe. He told me he was a doctor who had been in retirement when the war started, but had gone back to work because almost all the young doctors had been taken by the Army.

"I used to get awful tired and discouraged," he said, "but whenever I got real low I had a book I used to look at and it always made me feel better. It was called *Vermont Is Where You Find It.* Maybe you've heard of it?"

I was glad my face was all lathered up because I couldn't have stopped the instant tears. I told him that I had indeed heard of the book.

Emily was all in favor of the Rockland County move even though, as she pointed out, it involved a complicated trip across the Hudson twice a day for me to get to the office. So I went back to the big city, out to Rockland County and rented a large house that had three bad points for every good one. We moved our furniture in, and in an amazingly short time, out again. All in all we lived in five houses in the South Mountain Road area over the next twenty-five years.

In a curious, entirely unorganized way, South Mountain Road had been an artists' community since World War I. Henry Varnum Poor, Hugo Robus, Maxwell Anderson and others had built their houses on the twisting little road that led from High Tor west to the Ramapo hills. As the years went by other artists were drawn to the neighborhood including Edgar Levy and Lucille Corcos, Kurt Weill and Lotte Lenya, Morris Kantor and Martha Ryther.

Soon after we moved to the area, we began to be invited to the "road" gatherings. These would include famous names, unknowns and different crafts people in all fields. They were all friends and we were warmed by being included. I had learned a few chords on the guitar and had taken to singing some of the Burl Ives songs. At one party I was talking with Lenya and said that I would love to sing "September Song" but couldn't find the chords for it. The next morning she and Kurt stopped by the house with a copy of the sheet music, chords and all, and a best wishes note.

Some of the gatherings were at the home of Bunny and Milton Caniff—he of "Terry and the Pirates" and "Steve Canyon." Maybe the best bashes of them all were during the early years of Everett Crosby's High Tor vineyards. We would gather to pick the grapes during the long hot day and later sing and drink lots of last year's wine while a few pretty girls did some ceremonial grape stomping.

But the parties were incidental: what drew the group together and kept it together was respect for one another's work and the commitment of the artist to it.

Not too many of us from South Mountain Road commuted regularly to New York. Those of us who did used the dying West Shore Railroad which was thought by its conductors to be too good for the people who rode on it. The train took us to Weehawken where we crossed the river on a ferry and took a bus to midtown Manhattan. It was a long trip but considerably enlivened by the presence of highly compatible fellow sufferers: Mitch Miller from CBS Records, David Scherman and Joe Kastner from *Life,* Gil Burke from *Fortune,* one of my oldest friends Armon Glenn from *Barron's,* and other diverting folk.

Mitch Miller claimed that the group was invaluable to him. He frequently sought our opinions on his new releases and when we expressed unanimous loathing, as in the case of "I Saw Mommie Kissing Santa Claus," he said he knew he had a hit.

Everything was fine at H. Holt. We had published *Brave Men,* the second book of Ernie Pyle's dispatches, which was another tremendous hit, and Bill had managed another publishing coup by getting publication rights to the work of Bill Mauldin, whose drawings and cartoons of our infantrymen made them as real and understandable as Ernie Pyle's writings. Bill's book *Up Front* was a huge bestseller. Bill came out to live on South Mountain Road after the war. He bought his house from another author of ours who had moved to the West Coast—Marion Hargrove.

Over the years it has been fascinating to see how success changes writer's lives. Some writers are saved by their bestsellers and some are not. It's awfully hard for a writer who has just hit the jackpot to keep from adopting a life style that will need many more bestsellers to support it.

Many of us in the publishing business tried to keep the pressure on the people who wrote the tax codes to give authors of very profitable books tax breaks of a substantive kind. What we really wanted was the same depletion-of- resource breaks that the oil men were getting. We also lobbied for the same treatment for professional athletes, who did not have many years of high incomes any more than writers could duplicate their bestselling books. We did manage to accomplish a few helpful new statutes, but we didn't come close to getting what we wanted.

Not long after I had gotten back into the world of New York publishing a good deal of publicity broke about plans for a great Book Fair in Atlanta. It was to be a three-day celebration of books and authors. For a reason I never completely understood, I was invited to be the toastmaster for the opening night. I was complimented by the suggestion and accepted. I asked for a list of the authors

I would be introducing and began to do my homework on their backgrounds and accomplishments.

For my own part, I decided to tell a joke I had just heard, followed by an inspiring—to me anyway—paragraph which I memorized for the occasion, from Clarence Day's introduction to *The Story of the Yale University Press.*

The joke, which I felt to be peculiarly appropriate, was about a man who took his bear to the movies. One customer was so upset that he found the manager and pointed out the man and the bear sitting quietly watching the screen. The manager edged his way down the row behind them, struck the man on the shoulder, pointed to the bear and motioned them out.

When they reached the lobby the manager, almost incoherent with rage, asked the man what in the world he meant by bringing his bear into the movie theatre.

Somewhat puzzled, the man replied, "Well, he loved the book."

The Clarence Day paragraph went like this:

"The world of books is the most remarkable creation of man. Nothing else that he builds ever lasts. Monuments fall; nations perish; civilizations grow old and die out; and, after an era of darkness, new races build others. But in the world of books are volumes that have seen this happen again and again, and yet live on, still young, still as fresh as the day they were written, still telling the hearts of men centuries dead."

The night before the Fair's first day I boarded the train to Atlanta and, of course, ran into several friends bound for the Fair too. I had dinner with Lee Barker and John Selby. Lee Barker and Ken McCormick were chief editors of Doubleday and we had been friends for years. John Selby was an editor at Rinehart.

During our merry dinner Lee told me that he was to be toastmaster on the second night of the clambake. He said that since there were several Doubleday authors on the program for the first night why didn't he and I change nights. This was fine with me and I could use the time to do some work on the introductions of my new speakers. John Selby told us that he was the toastmaster for the children's book affair the afternoon of the second day. So we fell to talking about books and publishing in the club car and went too late to bed.

Then the next morning after breakfast I went to the Atlanta

library and made some notes for speakers presentations for the following night. I was delighted to see that John Mason Brown was on my program, although the idea of my introducing one of the most sought-after and wittiest speakers of the time seemed incongruous.

In the afternoon I called on several booksellers and talked a little business. The evening festivities started at eight and I was one of the first to be seated in the auditorium.

When I looked up to the stage my heart settled in my shoes. The whole back of the stage was the replica of a giant open book. Both pages were beautifully lettered in immense, lovely script. The left-hand page began with the words, "The world of books is the most remarkable creation of man..." My whole stirring, well-practiced creed. There went half my contribution. I had not begun to recover when the program began.

Lee Barker, my loyal comrade, stepped to the front of the stage and said, "Before I begin the formal part of tonight's program I want to tell a joke I heard in New York last week and I'm sure you will enjoy it. It seems that a man had a pet bear and one night he took him to the movies..."

He told the story very well and the audience loved it. I think I was the only person in the hall who didn't even smile.

John Selby decided to skip the opening night to prepare for his children's shindig the next afternoon. Not having heard Lee's opening to the first evening's entertainment, he told the bear story again.

That night I had a delightful dinner with John Mason Brown and told him about the subversion of my plans. John laughed and said he'd bet me ten dollars I didn't have guts enough to tell the bear story again. I didn't. But led by John's captivating remarks about life, the theater, his family and the life of a critic, the rest of my speakers were so good that I'm sure nobody noticed that I said almost nothing at all.

Under Bill Sloane's management the trade department of Henry Holt was going very well indeed. So well that Pat Lannon, a Chicago entrepreneur with literary tastes—he was a sponsor of *Poetry Magazine*—bought enough stock in the company to put him on the board of directors. As an admirer of Ernie Pyle, he had followed the other successes of the company.

A friend of Lannon's brought this news to the attention of Clint Murchison, who bought, sold and merged companies at a rate remarkable even for a Texas oil baron. Murchison had been wondering what to give his sons as college graduation presents and he thought that a New York book publishing house might be just the thing. He bought a controlling interest in Henry Holt and company and summoned Joe Brandt, who had succeeded Herbert Bristol as president, and Bill Sloane to Dallas for a conference.

Murchison informed the New Yorkers that his elder son would take over the business as soon as he graduated from college—a few months in the future, and that his second son would join him shortly thereafter. Joe and Bill talked with him for less than two hours and returned to New York with the conviction that a dismal future was in store for all of us.

The trade department, which now accounted for about 50 per cent of the gross business of the whole company, was a team, a unit, and gradually the concept of starting a new firm became more and more attractive. We explored ways to finance such a venture and the results were promising enough to announce the formation of a new firm called William Sloane Associates in March 1946. Helen Taylor, Norman Hood and I were Bill's partners. The rest of the Associates were assistant editors, our manufacturing man and several eager, talented younger people. Many friends in other publishing houses bought stock in ours.

Joe Brandt, naturally, didn't like the idea at all because it effectively left Henry Holt and Company without a trade department. He had a talk with me one day and said that if I wasn't completely committed to the new firm, which was as yet without financing, I could stay on at Holt as manager of the trade department.

I thanked him for the vote of confidence, but said that I was committed to the new firm. He didn't bring the matter up again.

I didn't think too much about my quick decision at the time, but many years later I realized that it defined exactly what role I wanted in publishing. I wanted to be part of the whole process, from selection through editing and design to the details of promotion and sales. I had never had any problems working within budget limits in advertising, sales and promotion, but I sensed that having the final financial responsibility would separate me from the product itself—that I would be working with accountants rather than authors and figures rather than manuscripts.

The new firm got off to a fine start. We worked for a while in a one-room office, then moved into half a floor in a building on West 57th Street. It seems hard to believe now, but one reason I was looking for office space on West 57th was because we had determined, on principle, never to have an all-white, all-gentile office. Even then in midtown New York it was hard for a black man or woman to find many restaurants that would serve them. The OWI had occupied a large building on West 57th, so most of the restaurants and coffee shops were used to having blacks and Hispanics as customers.

We were supported by a great deal of enthusiasm and good will from the beginning. And we were fortunate because our first list of publications contained Teddy White's *Thunder Out of China,* Nancy Wilson Ross's *The Left Hand is the Dreamer,* and A.B. Guthrie, Jr.'s *The Big Sky*—which almost won the Pulitzer Prize that was awarded to his next book, *The Way West.* We revitalized the *American Men of Letters* series and were rewarded by considerable prestige and the Carey Thomas Award for Creative Publishing.

We got more than our share of book club selections in our first two years, but I'll never forget how I heard about the first one.

I was in Chicago on a sales trip, part of which, naturally, involved taking two of our most important buyers out for a golf game. My partner in the match was Al Leventhal, one of the nicest and most brilliant men in publishing. He was part of Simon and Schuster's exciting crew which included, among others, Bob Gottlieb, Jack Goodman, Peter Schwed, Elinor Green and the best book advertiser ever, Nina Bourne.

Al and I were about to tee off on some hole and a club attendant whizzed up and said if one of us was Mr. Jennison there was an important telephone call for him at the clubhouse. It was a scary few minutes before I got to the phone. The call was from Bill Sloane telling me that the Book-of-the-Month had taken *Thunder Out of China* as a main selection.

I hurried back to the tee where I told Al, who owned stock in William Sloane Associates, the good news. Then I powered a drive about 280 yards straight down the fairway.

Al said, "There's nothing like a Book-of-the-Month selection to fix up your golf game."

There was always so much to learn from friends in other publishing houses. One of the things I learned from Al Leventhal was a mail-order test routine that was fascinating and baffling at the same time. Al would tool up a mail-order campaign on a book that had not yet been manufactured and do a test mailing—at two different prices. He said it was amazing how often he got more orders for the higher-priced version of exactly the same book. I asked him what happened when he got almost no orders for the book at either price. Al grinned and said they sent their apologies and a copy of a different book at a still higher price.

S & S was always coming up with innovative and almost always very saleable book projects. One of the most successful was a line of twenty-five cent books for children. The new series was called *Little Golden Books* and, of course, would have to sell in huge numbers to make the project profitable.

One of the first titles was *Doctor Dan the Bandage Man,* and M. Lincoln Schuster had an idea that it would be good merchandising to have a Band-Aid on the inside cover of each of the books. So he called the Executive Vice-President of Johnson & Johnson. According to an inside source the conversation went as follows:

"This is M. Lincoln Schuster of Simon and Schuster, book

publishers."

"Yes, Mr. Schuster, what can we do for you?"

"I'd like a price on two hundred and fifty thousand Band-Aids."

Johnson & Johnson was silent for a moment, then a friendly voice inquired, "What happened to you, Mr. Schuster?"

Mr. Schuster's answer was not recorded, but the tremendous success of *Little Golden Books* is well remembered.

One of our favorite stockholders was Everett DeGolyer, a very wealthy Texan who helped finance the *Saturday Review of Literature* and other literary enterprises. On my first business trip to Dallas I was invited out to his house for a party—a big and noisy one—but Mr. D. started showing me his library and by the time we rejoined the party it was over. The library spoke for the man. Both were impressive.

McMurray's Bookstore in downtown Dallas was, in many ways, the cultural center of Dallas. Liz Ann McMurray was interested in books, music, art; her best friend was Margo Jones, the famous drama producer in Dallas. They both were women of enormous energy who tended a creative bonfire that lit all Dallas. Somehow it didn't surprise me a bit to learn that one of Liz Ann's close friends, and future husband, was Bill Johnson, who was head of the *Time* office in Dallas. I had lost track of Bill since our London days and we had a fine reunion. I knew he had been *Time's* bureau chief in Argentina and Mexico, but I'd never heard any details about his adventures in those countries. He didn't write a book about Argentina, but he wrote two of the finest books on Mexico that have been published. I still remember Liz Ann's bookstore as the most exciting center of book retailing I ever called on.

In Houston I ran into the most frantic bookseller I ever met. The aisles of the store were crowded with planks set end to end on sawhorses. Clerks were taking books from the shelves and stacking them on the planks. Men, some in chauffeurs uniforms, would then pick up the stacks and rush them out to waiting limousines with open trunks.

The owner finally took a moment to tell me what was going on. An oilman had built a palatial residence, furnished it with priceless antiques, two Sisleys, one Van Gogh and many others, including a remarkable reproduction of Rembrandt's "Aristotle Gazing Upon the Bust of Homer." The Aristotle and Homer painting was naturally in the library. And this was the problem. Tonight was the official house warming for all the VIP's of Houston and the shelves of the library were empty. Somebody had forgotten to buy any books.

"First I started with all the most expensive limited editions I hadn't been able to sell, then all the biggest of the Abrams art books, after that a few hundred copies of books the publishers had refused to let me return." He stopped to take a deep breath.

"Then a whole bunch of current stuff that I shouldn't have taken into the store in the first place."

"Do you think you have enough books?" I intended this as humor.

"I'm not sure," he panted, "but when this is all over I'm going to close the store and take a week in San Francisco."

I had a wonderful time traveling around the country setting up commission sales coverages, going to Toronto and Montreal to learn how our Canadian representatives were going to schedule sales trips through their huge territory.

In 1947 my younger brother Peter, after finishing his tour of duty in WW II and graduating from Middlebury College, came to New York to look for a job in advertising or publishing. He went to work for Mildred Smith—editor of the *Publishers Weekly* and mother confessor to many members of the publishing fraternity—where he stayed until he was recruited by Ted Waller to join the staff of the American Book Publishers Council. It was great to have him in town even though we didn't see that much of each other. He served the industry with distinction both at home and abroad in many different capacities which led to his selection as the Executive Director of the National Book Committee. This committee was a blue-ribbon citizen's group devoted to "wiser and wider use of books in American life." It sponsored the National Book Awards and a useful spectrum of reading and library development programs. Along the way, Peter, having the same writing compulsion that I did, published two fine and well received novels, The Mimosa Smokers and The Governor."

The first two years at William Sloane Associates passed very quickly with things going so well that they seemed too good to be true. It turned out they were.

Our business manager had been sending the partners memos to

the effect that we needed more capital to finance our growth rate. When this matter came up in our directors' meetings Bill and the money men on the board advised us not to worry: the growth cycle would take care of that.

In 1949 Bill advised his partners that he had hired a college text executive to begin work on a college text publishing department of our own, and that he had signed an option to lease the rest of the floor of our building to house the future department.

Helen Taylor and I had a long talk with our business manager who showed us figures and projections that made the expansion seem much too risky. Rather, to our minds, the figures dictated some cuts in current overhead and the cancellation of some publishing projects that we had already scheduled. We reported our views to Bill, who suggested that we had grown faint of heart and would do well to adopt his creed of toujours l'audace.

After ten days of doing our own fiscal projections of estimated income and expenses, Helen and I wrote a letter to the board of directors saying that unless the firm delayed its expansion plans and cut back its operating expenses we would, with the utmost regret, submit our resignations.

We expected a board of directors meeting would be called to give us a chance to explain our position.

But that's not what happened. Bill called a directors meeting, but we were not notified of the time. The board voted to accept our resignations.

The months that followed were difficult and sad. Helen and I weren't sure what plans we wanted to make. Several authors told us privately they hoped we would start a publishing business of our own and they would be more than glad to give us their next books. Neither Helen nor I were convinced that this was the way we wanted to go, but in order to keep some kind of bargaining base with a new employer we announced that we were planning to start a new firm.

Almost immediately I had a call from Harold Guinzburg, who invited me to lunch. We talked about the Sloane situation and Harold agreed that we, as directors, had acted properly. He then said that if we wanted to set up our own firm he would subscribe half the capital we needed and that his friend, naming the owner of one of the largest book manufacturers, would put up the other half.

After some thought I said my only concern was that this arrangement would lock us into a single manufacturing source that would keep us from shopping around for price and quality. Harold said he'd talk to his friend about this and get back to us.

Helen and I were both delighted and apprehensive. We asked ourselves if we were good enough, and tough enough, to run a successful business of our own. While we waited for things to take shape, we worked out of a friend's apartment on manuscripts that interested us and cost projections that would enable us to specify how much capital we needed; how much cash and how much manufacturing credit— things like that.

We waited rather longer than we expected before Harold called us for a meeting. It was a much different meeting than the one we were prepared for.

Harold told us that there had been no problem about his friend having exclusive manufacturing rights to our books—he already has as much business as he could handle. All he wanted was his fair share.

This sounded fine. Then we got down to the real obstacle. Harold's friend said that he didn't care how much capital the new firm would need, but he insisted that he own one percent more of it than Harold did.

It was hard for us to understand this particular money game the old friends were playing but apparently neither would give an inch—or a percent. Harold thought his friend was behaving ridiculously in the matter and said he wasn't going to let him get away with it. We thought this was the end of the lunch, but Harold had something else to offer.

"Do you two really insist on having your own firm?" he asked.

We said we didn't.

"Then why don't you both just move into Viking? We'd love to have you both and your publishing programs."

Helen and I looked at each other. We didn't have to go away and discuss the pros and cons. Viking was a publisher of the highest quality and reputation. We felt honored to be asked to become a part of it and agreed on the spot. Helen was to become full-time editor and I a half-time editor and a half-time promotion manager. We both were to be members of the editorial board.

I was angered and heartsick by the William Sloane Associates experience. Bill and I were still neighbors in the country, commuting on the same trains, and going to the same parties. Our alienation was an embarrassment to our friends and neighbors and a hardship for ourselves. After a few months our temperatures returned to normal, and we picked up our friendship from where we had dropped it. We found it bruised but unbroken.

It was no satisfaction three years later to learn that William Sloane Associates had been sold and would operate as an imprint of William Morrow and Company. Bill went to Funk and Wagnalls as Vice-President and Executive Editor where, among other books, he published my first novel. Later, Bill became Director of the Rutgers University Press where he published many distinguished books. He remained there until his death in 1974.

In the spring of 1950, while final arrangements were being made to join Viking, I was invited to participate in a kind of literary forum at the University of Vermont. Jack Aldridge, of the UVM faculty, was the leader and the panel consisted of Malcolm Cowley, Mary McCarthy, Allen Tate, Carl Carmer and myself. It was a day-long affair and the discussion of writing in general, writing in particular, literary criticism in theory and practice was on a very high level indeed, and I thought it best to keep my silence until a man stood up and asked in an exasperated voice, "What's wrong with reading mysteries?"

Up to that point my fellow panel members had been quick to raise a hand indicating that the question from the floor was one which he or she would like to comment on. This time no hand went up until I raised mine.

The question and the tone of voice in which it was asked challenged me to try to put in words my thinking on the matter of the aesthetic experience.

I said that there was nothing whatever wrong with reading mysteries. Reading a book, I said, looking at a picture or listening to music causes a state of mind. If the state of mind can be called good or valuable, then the book, picture or music is good or valuable.

"Suppose I read a book and don't like it," the man said, "does that mean it's a bad book?"

I knew that one was coming. "No, all it means is that you didn't like it."

"About this state of mind," a lady asked from the floor, "you wouldn't by any chance have a definition for it would you?"

I felt like saying that if I didn't have a definition for that I would have kept my hand in my pocket.

"I think that a state of mind can be called good or valuable to the degree (underlined by my voice) that it tends to reduce a feeling of waste and frustration."

Carl Carmer spoke up. "Are you saying that the better a book makes you feel the better the book is?"

"Yup, but just for you. Might be different for somebody else."

"What about the intrinsic value of a work of art?" Jack Aldridge asked.

"Materials and technique only," I said, "all art aims at communicating feeling."

"He's just quoting Tolstoy," Mary McCarthy said.

I was, and Jack Aldridge thought we better move along to another area of discussion.

When the meeting was over it turned out that Miss McCarthy didn't have a room for the night. There was some talk of motels, but I suggested that since I was only twenty-five miles from my ancestral home she might do worse than to come home with me and I would drive her back down to the Burlington airport in the morning.

She accepted, we started off in our veteran Chevrolet and two miles later, in the center of Winooski, the car groaned, the engine stopped and we coasted to a halt in front of what looked like a combination filling station, garage and bar.

Winooski, Vermont in 1950 was not a garden spot. The days of its river-powered affluence were long gone and it was now no more than a shabby suburb of Burlington. But the young mechanic at the garage was eager and seemed to be competent. He looked at the engine and told me what had gone wrong. I didn't understand a word of the diagnosis: all I wanted to know was how long it would take to fix it.

"An hour, maybe," he said. "You could have a beer in the saloon there."

That seemed sensible to both of us. The bar was dingy but the draft beer was good and cold.

"You didn't talk much during the meeting," Mary said. I agreed.

She went on, "I got the idea you don't think very much of most literary criticism. Did you ever read any of mine?"

I admitted that I hadn't.

"Or my ex-husband's?"

"Well yes, I liked Mr. Wilson's criticism, but I liked *Memoirs of Hecate County* better."

"So did he, in a way. Let's have another beer."

We talked about publishing for a while and she said I was lucky to be going to Viking for a number of reasons, not the least of which was that I would be working with Pascal Covici. She had gone to work for Pat in 1936 and liked and respected him greatly.

Suddenly she asked, "Why did you bring up that art as communication stuff at the seminar?"

"For a long time I've been thinking about readers feeling guilty about not liking books that they were told they ought to like. I've read pretty widely and I came up with a concept that I liked. In the words of an advertising friend of mine I thought I'd run it up the flag pole and see if anybody saluted."

"I didn't."

"I noticed."

"All you're really saying is the old 'beauty is in the eye of the beholder' concept and that isn't very much to say."

I'd dealt with this charge before. "It all depends on how you spell "eye."

"What?"

"In that line I spell it with a capital I—you know, the old vertical pronoun."

"Meaning what?"

"The I of the beholder is the whole person—at whatever stage of intellectual and emotional development he's reached at the time of going through a particular aesthetic experience."

"Doesn't your beholder have any responsibility, or is it okay if he just keeps on liking the same old crap?"

"Of course he's got a responsibility, if to nothing else except his own pleasure. If the reader has any sense at all he'll start to identify what he liked best in a reading experience and begin to look for more of it. The more he asks of the time he spends reading the sooner he'll find the writers who deliver the most of what he likes."

"For example...?"

I told her about an English professor friend of mine who had a young student who hated the assigned classics he was forced to read. A friend asked him what he liked to read. The young man told him, somewhat defensively, that he liked Jacland Marmur's sea stories in the *Saturday Evening Post*. My friend suggested he try reading some Conrad. A couple of weeks later he asked if he could do a book report on *Typhoon* because he had liked it so much.

Just then the young man came in and said that the car was ready.

"I won't salute," Mary said, "but I will nod in your direction."

Working at Viking was a delight from the very beginning. Upon my arrival, I was told that Ben Huebsch was away on his annual trip to London and I was to use his office for a few weeks.

Ben Huebsch was one of the most beloved and respected men in American book publishing. Ben was a gentle, courtly man who had been an independent publisher since World War I. His small firm had published *Portrait of the Artist as a Young Man* by James Joyce in 1915, D.H. Lawrence's poetry, Sherwood Anderson's *Winesburg, Ohio* and his magazine *The Freeman* had published H.L. Mencken. When he joined Viking in 1925 he brought with him a young Harvard man, Marshall Best, and two young lady assistants. One of them told me that when things used to get slow in their office Mr. Huebsch would sometimes take them to an afternoon matinee or a Philharmonic concert.

The first few days it was difficult for me to feel comfortable sitting at his desk in his chair.

Ben was Editor-in-Chief of Viking when I got there, and Marshall Best was chairman of the executive committee. Helen and I brought five books with us and they all were successfully published under the Viking imprint. The authors were delighted and so were we.

Getting to know the fine people at Viking was one of the great pleasures of my life. Jack Mullen, the sales manager, was the only one I had known before, but it didn't take long for me to feel at ease with everyone there.

I suppose the one who became dearest to me over the years was

Mary McCarthy's friend Pascal Covici. Pat had been a Chicago bookseller and publisher of national recognition. He had been John Steinbeck's first publisher and his list was studded with other writers of the highest caliber.

I liked getting to the office early but most of the time Pat was there before I was. Sometimes our early talks were serious discussions of manuscripts and projects that were coming up for decision, but more often small talk of one kind or another.

One morning I told Pat that I had just heard that he was Rumanian. Pat said that was true.

"Then you're the one who can tell me what the real difference is between a Rumanian and a Hungarian."

"That's easy," Pat said. "They both will sign a contract agreeing to sell you their mother but the Rumanian will deliver."

"I don't know about that," I said, "I can't tell whether that's an anti-Hungarian or an anti-Rumanian joke."

"Doesn't matter," Pat said. "Everybody knows about Hungarians."

"Knows what?"

"They can't be trusted with money," Pat said, "and besides they're terrible tightwads. The biggest pinch penny of them all is right here in New York.

"Molnàr," Pat said, "Ferenc Molnàr the great playwright. He's the only Hungarian refugee with any money and he's a cheapskate."

Pat, with great relish, told me that a group of Hungarians had a little luncheon group that met every day at a special Third Avenue deli. Money was a constant topic of conversation for several years after the war because many of the refugees had families that were in need, but under the currency law they were unable to send money home, even if they got their hands on some.

"Molnàr joined this group every day," Pat said, "but he wouldn't order anything. He'd take bites from his friends' sandwiches and drinks from their beer glasses. Nobody objected because he was the famous Molnàr. One day he was very late to lunch and his friends began to worry. Finally he showed up with his shirt pulled open and sweat showing on his pale, stricken face. He stood, trembling, beside the table.

"Have you heard the terrible news from Hungary?" His voice was weak.

"No Ferenc, no. What? What?"

His eyes swept the group in desperation, "We can now send money!"

Pat was very much a part of John Steinbeck's life and saw to it that I had a chance to spend time with John at various formal and informal gatherings. It was through Pat that I got to know Arthur Miller, Gene Fowler and Saul Bellow.

The Viking advisory editor was Malcolm Cowley, whose poetry and criticism I had admired for years. His book *The Lost Generation* seemed to me to be the best by far of all the writings on the post-World War I writers. Malcolm came in every Tuesday for the editorial meetings and for a lunch with Marshall Best and Pat and sometimes me.

Marshall was Harold Guinzburg's right-hand man—a stickler for detail who insisted that everything we did, we did well. Somehow, for example, he made time to read carbon copies of all outgoing mail.

I can remember the shock and quick anger I felt when a phrase in a letter of mine was queried or edited. It took me quite a while before I noticed that every change made for a clearer, better letter. He was a hard man to get to know. He seemed not to encourage it. But I liked and admired him and after about five years, in a halting and somewhat embarrassed way, he let me know that he valued my friendship.

There were many others in whose debt I shall always be. Milton Glick, for what he taught me about design and manufacturing. May Massee, the best known and admired children's book editor in the business, for showing me, by example, how a children's book department ought to be run. Alice Roberts of the copy-editing department, for making it clear that no detail, however small, should be overlooked. And Ben Huebsch who taught me how tough and uncompromising a gentle man could be.

Back out in Rockland County I had been seeing a most attractive Englishman who had served in the Indian Army—the sixth generation of his family to do so. He had decided that he and his wife and children had a more attractive future in the United

States than in either India or Great Britain. His name was John Masters and he had a distinguished war record. I knew that he had written one or more books that had not found publishers, but I hadn't asked to see them due to my concern for the future of William Sloane Associates. But now that I was at Viking it was part of my job to find publishable manuscripts.

At that point Jack had two "finished" manuscripts. His first was an autobiography called *Brutal and Licentious,* which had been turned down by a dozen publishers. The second, *Nightrunners of Bengal,* was sharing the same fate.

Jack was a lean, hawk-faced six-footer with dark eyes under heavy brows. He was tough, disciplined, unemployed and broke. Soon after our first talk I learned that he was being coached in the skills of ironing and cooking so his wife Barbara could take a secretarial job.

Our first talk was the most extraordinary conversation I ever had with an author. Jack told me that when he had decided to try to make a living by writing he must concentrate on the things he knew the most about. For Jack, this meant India and soldiering. He had been trained by Sandhurst and the army to make battle plans that were complete in every detail. This experience resulted in a writing plan that was like no other writer's projections that I had ever heard of.

Jack had decided to write a panel of thirty-five novels that would, when completed, tell the whole story of the British in India—all 300 years of it. He had taken a map of India, made one transparent overlay of the locations of the key events in this history and another overlay which represented the genealogy of his fictional family named Savage. By looking through the two transparencies to the places on the map you could tell which of the family had been involved in the major actions that had shaped India.

It was a wonderfully impressive plan and his military record proved that when he was given an assignment, or had made one for himself, he carried through with complete dedication.

He left a copy of the *Nightrunners of Bengal* manuscript with me because I had said that I thought the autobiography might perform much better after he became known as a successful novelist.

136

I read it and knew it was a book whose publication I would push hard for. I thought it needed some additional work in different sequences, but nothing that would add up to a major rewrite. I took it to Helen to read and she felt the same way. We told Jack that we liked it very much, but we'd like him to do some more work on it before we put it through the Viking selection process. He agreed, and later, in a volume of autobiography, he was to write, "She [Helen Taylor] was a big blond woman, craggy and kind. I still think she was the best editor in New York, and this not only because she was my first, when I needed one the most and had the most to learn."

Jack and Helen worked on the manuscript for almost six months. Barbara Masters retyped it and I started to get some readings from Viking editors. The weeks passed and I was surprised that the readers' reports were not very enthusiastic. By this time I had learned the strategy and tactics of the editorial meeting.

Early every Tuesday morning the editorial secretary came to each of the senior editors and asked if he or she had something to bring up at the meeting. The list was mimeographed and each of us had a copy at our place at the long oval table in the Viking library.

An editor would bring up a book, describe it, quote from readers' reports and there would be a general discussion. A book was rarely taken after only one meeting of the board. I had learned that when I brought up a book I was doubtful about, or maybe in a sneaky way didn't really like, I would change my mind and agree with one or two editors who would say that it was a fairly good project, but not one for Viking.

Upon occasion I'd do this twice in the same meeting, accepting the rejection of a project with mild dissent. Then I'd go after one I really wanted.

I've forgotten how many editorial meetings Jack Master's first novel went through, but it was more than five. I didn't bring it up every week; that would have been fatal. When I did put it on the agenda and the comments made me realize that if I pressed for a decision it would be negative, I'd back off and say, "Well, let's let it go for now and talk about it again sometime."

In the end the matter was not settled in the meeting at all. I had a meeting with Harold and Marshall one day and made a serious explanation of why we should take this book and especially why we should take on this author.

Marshall said, "But we've never published anything like this before and we don't really know how good it is."

As impressively as I could I said, "I do."

Harold turned to Marshall and said, "Maybe he's right. Let's go ahead with it."

We published Jack's book to considerable acclaim from critics and other writers. The Literary Guild bought the book-club rights thereby enabling Jack immediately to discontinue his ironing classes.

Over the following five years we published five more of Jack's books. His wonderful first volume of autobiography—*Brutal and Licentious,* which had been turned down by almost every New York publisher—was brought out with the title *Bugles and a Tiger.* It was taken by the Book-of- the-Month Club and welcomed by readers and critics.

The four novels included perhaps his best-known novel, *Bhowani Junction,* which was made into a memorable motion picture. His last novel for Viking was *Far, Far the Mountain Peak,* which had both disappointing sales and disappointing reviews. Jack decided that a change of publishers would do him no harm and might do him some good. There was no break in our friendship, but we saw less and less of each other in Rockland County. In a few years Jack and Barbara were living in New Mexico and Emily and I saw them not at all.

Whenever a publisher loses an author he has nurtured and published with great mutual success it is a blow. But the lesson that we have to learn is to keep the same perception, enthusiasm and commitment ready for the next would-be novelist who excites our attention.

There were so many great days during my years at Viking that it's hard to single out ones that were all that much more special. I was deeply involved in most of the operations of Viking—except financial. One important area was relations with authors.

One of Viking's most colorful authors was Gene Fowler, who was thought by many to be the greatest reporter in American journalism. Gene finally gave up his tumultuous newspaper career and wrote movie scripts and several very successful volumes of biography. His writings are humorous, compassionate, irreverent celebrations of life. The best known is probably his biography of John Barrymore, *Goodnight, Sweet Prince,* a best-seller and one which was hailed by a critic as the best biography of an actor ever written.

Gene had severe limitations as a biographer. He couldn't write the story of a person he didn't like, know well and think of as a friend. In 1951 we published his biography of Jimmy Durante, the ever-popular comic entertainer, whose tours and radio appearances had made him a great favorite across the country. Everybody loved him and Gene most of all. His book was wonderful fun to read.

I planned a publication-day celebration that would help get the book off to a good start. First there was to be a tour of six or seven bookstores where Jimmy would greet fans and Gene would auto-graph his books. Late in the afternoon there was to be a reception for the New York book trade and reviewers at Toots Shor's famous watering hole.

When I phoned Jimmy from the lobby of his hotel he told me to come up; he hadn't dressed or had breakfast. He was half-dressed by the time I got to his room. We were running late and I worried about what the breakfast procedure would be. I needn't have. He finished dressing in minutes, took six brown eggs out of a dresser drawer, broke them one by one into a large glass and downed the contents in three gulps.

He gave me his enchanting grin. "Never have anything else. Let's go."

I had no notion of what it would be like to ride around New York in a taxi with Gene Fowler and Jimmy Durante. Every cab driver we had knew either one or both of my companions. Not one driver would take money.

The autographing sessions at the bookstores, especially Macy's, were miniature mob scenes, and when we finally arrived at Toots Shor's we found that our gang had almost taken over the place.

As soon as we appeared Jimmy was carried to the piano where he sang his famous theme, "Ink-a-Dink-a-Doo" and other favorites from the days when the act of Clayton, Jackson and Durante was getting top billing in vaudeville houses from coast to coast.

The party ended with Eddie Jackson at the piano singing "Won't You Come Home, Bill Bailey" to applause that rattled the glasses on the bar.

Over the next few years Pat Covici, knowing how much I was attracted to Gene, made sure that whenever Gene came to New York I got to spend some time with him. I knew from his books that he had been liked and admired by Mr. Hearst, who had succeeded in getting Gene to take the job of being managing editor of the *New York American*. Gene didn't like the job very much, nor Mr. Hearst either, but he stuck with it as long as he could. His fellow newspapermen had great affection and regard for Gene and proved it in an almost unbelievable way.

Gene had been in a long evening conference with Mr. Hearst discussing an almost complete reorganization of the Hearst newspaper chain—names, cities, editors, firings, hirings, all the explosive details.

Gene didn't think the plan was a good one and told the great man so. Mr. Hearst asked Gene to take the thick file home with him, study it and come back for further debate.

Gene told me this story at Pat's apartment one night. "So I took the file, grabbed a cab and went to a bar hanging on to the most secret document I'd ever been responsible for. I had a few drinks and took another cab home. As the cabbie pulled away I realized I'd left the file in the cab."

He told a newspaper friend of his predicament. This friend told another, "And pretty soon," Gene said, "half the newsmen in the city were looking for that damn file. They called all the cab companies and got drivers' trip sheets. Finally one of them found the driver, tracked him to his home in Brooklyn and went to see him.

"As soon as he got into the man's living room, he saw the floor was covered by sheets of the file. The man had given them to his kids to draw on." Gene shook his head in wonder, "And then he returned them to me...all of them...unread...the hottest story in years."

In another evening session of trading memories, opinions, likes and dislikes Gene told me of the long struggle he had had trying to finish a biography of W.C. Fields. He had worked on it for years, written a carton of notes but couldn't get it into the shape he wanted. Finally, hearing that Robert Lewis Taylor had begun work on a Fields biography, Gene shipped all of his notes off to Taylor with the invitation to use whatever he wanted. Taylor's book was published in 1949 and received generally good reviews with the exception of one which said that the book was fine but not as well written as Gene Fowler's books.

At one such session Gene started telling Barrymore stories that weren't in his book. One dialogue, as reported by Gene, may illustrate why it was left out.

"Jack and I were talking about how lovely his sister Ethel was when she was a young woman. Jack said that at one time in England she was being wooed simultaneously by Winston Churchill and Edward VII. I had heard rumors of these goings-on for a long time, but there was a direct question I had never asked." Gene paused to fix his drink.

"I said, 'Jack, did your sister ever lay Edward the Seventh?'"

"Jack said, 'Did she not...she had beard burns on her breasts for months.'"

When Barrymore was dying he insisted that Gene come to his bedside. Gene leaned close to hear his dying words.

"Tell me," Barrymore whispered, "is it true you are the illegitimate son of Buffalo Bill?"

One of Gene's favorite friends in New York was Jack Dempsey, and often when Gene was in town we went to Dempsey's restaurant for lunch or dinner, always sitting at Jack's table. To listen to old friends talk about fights and fighters that were legends to me was a very special experience.

Gene once wrote of himself, "The escapades of Mr. Fowler were many and his moral guilt was grave—according to worldly standards but not to his own. He refused all his life to be a secret drinker, a secret lecher and a secret wisher for forbidden fruits... he was too lazy to erect screens and too proud to pretend chastity when there was no chastity in his soul."

The year before Gene died in 1960, *Holiday Magazine* printed a piece about him by Lucius Beebe which contained the following paragraph:

"No man living and only a few of those who have joined the majority have better claim to the honored sword and cloak of journalism in the romantic dimension. A legend in his Park Row lifetime, Fowler is now an immortal, full of the juices of turmoil and of understanding and still walking the earth, an envied repository of great days gone, who has by no means spent his last shaft."

Everyone in American publishing had seen the paperback "revolution" coming and by the early 1950's many hundreds of millions of pocket-size paperback books were being sold. We at Viking had never thought of ourselves as publishers of books for the mass market, so our entrance into the paperback field took two different forms. The first line consisted of "quality" paperbacks printed from the original plates which would fit into a pocket only if the pocket were oversized. By "quality" we meant that the titles were, in our opinion, of permanent interest to one or more of the individual audiences that made up the book market. These we called *Compass Books*.

In the 1940's Viking had established the *Viking Portable Library*, consisting of volumes made up of representative works of a favorite modern or classic author and comprehensive anthologies of special subjects. These books were beautifully designed and printed on thin paper and ran to five or six-hundred pages. They were thought by many to be the best bargains in books available at the time. These fine, fat little books would fit in an ordinary jacket pocket provided there was nothing else in the pocket.

There were sixty or seventy titles in the series which offered reading of all kinds in the works of the best-known writers of the ages. Each volume had a new introduction by a contemporary critic that added richness and depth to the reading experience.

It had always seemed to me, and I'm sure to all book lovers, that one of the most precious qualities of a book was that you could always keep it available—to be read where and when you felt like it. Upstairs, downstairs, indoors, outdoors, lying down, sitting up, on a plane, bus, train—anywhere. You could read at the speed you liked, going back and rereading if you cared to. Somewhere in my reading I had run across a quotation from Richard de Bury who wrote in 1345, "These are the masters who instruct us without whip or rod, without harsh words or anger, asking naught in return. If you seek them, they are not asleep; if you ask counsel of them, they do not refuse it; if you go astray they do not chide; if you betray ignorance to them they know not how to laugh in scorn. Truly of all our teachers Books alone are free and freely teach."

This quotation came often to my mind whenever censors, reformers, bigots and chauvinists tried to curb the free production and distribution of books.

The nature of the publishing business was always changing— sometimes subtly, other times dramatically and suddenly. For many years the annual reports on the book publishing industry showed that the basic product—the book—was being produced and distributed at 102 per cent of cost. Of course this figure made bankers and economists think we were all crazy or incompetent. The simple answer was that if, say, a particular publisher had an annual gross of $10,000,000 about 10 per cent of this figure would have been created by the publisher's share of income from special rights—movie sales, book club selections, paperback reprint rights, anthology use, foreign sales and dramatizations. This income came to the publisher and was then split with the author according to the percentages specified in the contract.

When I first went to Harcourt, Brace I recall being surprised that if a book club paid HB $75,000 for the right to print an edition for their members the author got 50 per cent of the payment. This was an industry-wide practice at that time. The rationalization was that the publisher needed his share to show a net profit after all his regular sales at 102 per cent of cost.

When authors complained about this distribution of funds that his or her book had created, the publishing response was that the author was part of a national literary fellowship and that since most publishers showed a loss on at least one out of every three books they published, the writer of the successful book had a moral responsibility to see to it that fine books kept on being published whether they made money or not.

Some authors accepted this justification and some didn't. The issue came up more and more frequently in the 1950's. Literary agents, who represented their clients' natural desire to make as much money as they could, fought harder and harder for changing the participation percentages. Little by little the balance changed to favor the writer.

What this meant from a publishing standpoint was that the publisher had less money to publish, say, a poet whose book would not come close to breaking even in the marketplace, even though it was poetry of the finest quality and was memorable and rewarding for hundreds of—but not enough—people.

I remember well a scene with the bankers of William Sloane Associates who asked us how many books we were going to publish in the following year.

Bill said, "About sixty."

Our leading banker said, "How many of them are you going to make money on?"

"About forty," Bill said, "if we're lucky."

The banker looked dumbfounded. "Then what are you publishing the other twenty for?"

Bill gave him the only answer we had: "Because we don't know which ones they are."

The pressure to publish only bestsellers kept increasing as costs went up and conglomerate hunters appeared on the scene. All of us tried to reduce our overhead costs. Many firms reduced their editorial staffs.

For many years there had been behavior codes in the book publishing business that made about as much business sense as an over-zealous adherence to the Golden Rule.

One did not seek to buy a successful author away from his present publisher. If an author decided he'd be happier with another publisher and came to us to inquire if we were interested in taking him on, we didn't ask his reasons, but we did ask for details of his contractual commitments, if any, to his current publisher. Usually we called the current publisher to let him know what was going on.

Three years after I had sold the hardbound reprint rights to Ernie Pyle's *Here Is Your War,* Donald Grosset of Grosset and Dunlap, called on me at William Sloane Associates. He asked me if I remembered the telephone conversation about his original guarantee of $50,000.

I said I did.

"Do you remember saying that if we didn't make the guarantee you wouldn't hold us to it?"

I said I did and asked him how much they had missed it by.

"That's not the point," Donald said, "it was just under three thousand dollars, but all the directors of Henry Holt and Company want to know is whether you remember saying you'd let us off the hook if we didn't make the guarantee."

"You mean the directors feel that when I told you that I was speaking for Henry Holt and Company?"

"That's it."

"Well, good for them," I said. "Sam Goldwyn was wrong."

"What about Sam Goldwyn?"

"Sam Goldwyn said that a verbal agreement wasn't worth the paper it was written on."

Of course we didn't make verbal agreements that involved specific sums of money. Payments were specified in written contracts. As the years passed the contracts got longer and longer—but not necessarily clearer or more binding. It took me quite a while to understand that a contract was really no better than the intent of the people who signed it. Our company lawyers were paid not to win court cases but to keep us from having any.

The more I saw of Malcolm Cowley the more impressed I was with his total involvement with writing, editing and lecturing in various parts of the country and his abiding interest in responding to talented writers wherever he found them—or they found him.

Somewhere on his travels Malcolm had met a writer, part American Indian, who said he had a manuscript he'd like a publisher to look at. Malcolm gave him the Viking address and when the book came in I read it before anyone else. The book was called *Stay Away, Joe* and was about the trials and tribulations of a young not-so-brave Indian. I found the book touching, hilarious and sadly revealing about the current culture of a group of original Americans. Malcolm was away, so I brought the book to the attention of the other editors along with my enthusiastic insistence that we publish it.

We did publish it with great success. The Book-of-the- Month Club took it, reprinters competed for the paperback rights and one day I discovered that I was getting credit for having "discovered" the author. I brought this up with Malcolm and said I didn't think it was fair. He had found the author and, for what it was worth, should get the credit for it. He said he had forgotten about the whole incident of meeting the author until after he had read the finished book. He said it didn't matter who read it first. All that mattered was that a good book had had a good publishing job done on it.

At this time Malcolm had been working with a wild young writer named Jack Kerouac, whose first novel, *The Town and the City* had been published in 1950 by my old friend Bob Giroux at

Harcourt Brace and Company. Jack was an explosive experimenter with all the aspects of being alive, as well as being an undisciplined, compulsive writer about his visions and perceptions. Malcolm saw enormous talent in Jack and worked hard to try to get more of Jack's writing into print.

A most exciting new author to come to Viking in the 1950's was Saul Bellow. Part of the arrangement through which he came to us was our re-publication of his two brilliant novellas, *The Dangling Man* and *The Victim*, in the *Compass* paperback line.

Saul was a wonderfully attractive, feisty man whose first novel for us was *The Adventures of Augie March*, an irresistible tale of a young man's attempt to discover if there was any significance in the human experience and, if so, what it was. As a writer Saul shared a quality with Isaac Bashevis Singer, that of being always a serious writer but never a solemn one.

They both won Nobel prizes.

When I finished reading Augie March I was sure it was going to be a bestseller. All the elements were there: a new novel by an author certified to be important by critics and whose work one ought to read and admire. When this factor was combined with an appealing protagonist in a series of events and escapades that readers would find constantly engaging, the result was predictable.

The reviews were all very good indeed, but there was a note of condescension in a few of them that infuriated me. These were reviews that hinted Augie was fine and all that, but when was the author going to tackle a book that was worthy of his talents?

One day I was in Pat Covici's office and we were reading a review of Augie in one of the leading journals of literary criticism. Much of the review was taken up with an admiring examination of the way Bellow used symbols. As an example, the critic cited a section of the novel that told the story of the adventures of Augie in Mexico with a man and wife who trained hunting eagles. It was a superb re-creation of gorgeous scenery and the methods by which eagles were trained to hunt. One of the young eagles, however, apparently didn't want to be a hunting eagle. All he wanted to do was soar and circle through the sky with no thought, apparently, of learning how to kill anything.

The critic applauded Bellow's use of this metaphor of the reluctant eagle to define the author's own instincts.

Pat and I were talking about the review when Saul walked into the office and joined us. We gave him the review to read. When he finished he looked up with a puzzled expression.

"I don't know what the fuck he's talking about. I'm just using Augie to tell about a trip I made with Dan and Sylvia Mannix who have been training eagles all over the world. We had a ball in Mexico. The weather was great and so was the beer."

The next few years at Viking were so packed with exciting and fulfilling work that it's hard for me to recall the sequence of some of the situations, people and happenings that remain so vivid in my mind.

I guess the point was that Viking had a single standard for its publishing procedures. You worked just as hard and carefully on a book by, say, Dagmar Godowski as you did on a book by Graham Greene.

I was the first reader of an untitled autobiography by a woman with the name Dagmar Godowski. My first thought was, "Who the hell is Dagmar Godowski?" My second thought was what a wonderful title that would make if we ended up publishing the book.

I read the manuscript at one sitting. It was colorful, fascinating and full of anecdote. We did publish it—but not under the title I fought for. Dagmar had a sense of humor, but it didn't cover that specific title.

Dagmar was the daughter of the world-renowned pianist Leopold Godowski, and had a movie career as a wicked vamp second only to Theda Bara—according to Theda, not Dagmar.

Dagmar and her sister were brought up in the family mansion in Leipzig which, according to Dagmar, was the center of cultural life in the city. There were endless parties, receptions, concerts and dinner parties to which the little girls were not invited, although they did spy from the top of the great staircase.

On one occasion, feeling particularly neglected and resentful, the girls watched the preparations for a grand dinner party. When the servants had completed the intricate and impressive table setting with a magnificent flower arrangement in the center, Dagmar had an idea. She told her sister what it was and her sister agreed to play her part in the plan.

The girls knew that for about an hour before the guests were summoned to dinner the dining room was empty. The servants were all making last-minute preparations elsewhere.

During this time the girls sneaked into the room, crept under the table and managed to separate the center leaves just enough for their purpose. Dagmar had brought a pair of scissors and a chair from the children's playroom. She moved the flower arrangement to one side, cut a round hole in the tablecloth and placed the little chair directly beneath it. Dagmar then seated her sister in the chair and guided her head up through the hole and arranged the flowers around it.

When their parents and their guests entered the dining room the result was everything the girls had wished for.

For a few years Dagmar's family lived in a splendid apartment on New York's Fifth Avenue. The apartment provided a two-story balconied ballroom. Dagmar wrote about one party for which the floor had been laid out in 30 inch black and white squares. The guests were instructed to come dressed as chess pieces. Her father stood on the balcony at one end, arranged his guests in the proper positions and, as host, made the opening move. His opponent at the other end of the hall was Sergei Rachmaninov.

A good deal of publishing business in New York was done during meals. Business lunches, cocktails and dinners were pleasant venues for getting acquainted, agreeing on contracts and having editorial discussions.

There were two pretty well defined editorial practices. One was the European custom of leaving an author's work exactly as he wrote it. Ben Huebsch was known to have refused to let a copy editor change an error in fact in a manuscript because that was the way the author had written it. The American approach varied greatly from editor to editor. Some editors had the unfortunate habit of taking the position that if he or she were writing the sentence, paragraph, chapter or book he or she wouldn't have done it that way. The great New York editors worked from the premise that the editor and author worked together to ask more of the book than would ever again be asked by any reader or critic. There were many non-confrontational ways to help a writer seek his highest performance level. You couldn't tell him how to do it, but your enthusiasm and confidence could contribute to his ability to find it in himself.

At one lunch with a couple of editor friends we blasted the degeneration of standards in the use of our language. As the use of written communication declined in the wake of electronic developments, grammar got sloppier all the time. Of course the Churchill story of how he reacted to a copy editor's correction of one of his sentences which ended with a preposition was mentioned.

Churchill had changed the sentence back to the way he had written it. His marginal note read, "This is the kind of nonsense up with which I will not put."

One member of our lunch said he could give us a sentence that ended in five prepositions. We challenged him to do so.

"A man," the story began, "went up to his son's room at bedtime with a book in his hand. As he stood at the bedroom door the boy looked up and said, 'Why did you bring that book that I don't want to get read to out of up for?'"

The way our language was being used was changing, of course, and to our ears and standards very much for the worse. But then, it always had changed, and usage always became the arbiter. I sometimes wondered how the literary community had felt about the way language changed between the poetry of Chaucer and the plays of Shakespeare.

I admired my friends who were fighting the tide of insensitive degradation of the way we spoke and wrote, but I couldn't remember whether Canute drowned or just got wet.

At one luncheon seminar we mourned the passing of the use of the subjunctive. Harvey Breit, of *The New York Times,* was with us that day and said that he loved that particular verb form, but that every time he used it his editor changed it. Harvey's column in the *Times Book Review* was widely read and liked and it seemed unbelievable that this kind of editing was going on.

Harvey said he was going to get a subjunctive past the little, beady eyes of his persecutor by some method.

We bet him he couldn't. Several weeks later Harvey's column contained a big, beautiful subjunctive. The next time he joined us for lunch we asked him how he had done it.

"Simple," Harvey said, "I sneaked down to the composing room, found the compositor who had my copy and changed the editor's verb to mine. Pay up."

At Viking, as indeed at all publishing houses, we had authors with radically differing personalities. Some were quiet, intense and inward, far more interested in writing than they were in being writers. Others were extroverted to the point of celebrating their writerhood in gaudy and sometimes infuriating conduct.

One of Viking's more colorful authors was Ludwig Bemelmans, an Austrian-born restauranteur, hotel manager, artist, entrepreneur, and writer and illustrator of books. He was a round, bouncy man with enormous enthusiasms for eating, drinking, partying, working and promoting Ludwig Bemelmans.

His famous books featuring a little French girl named Madeleine made him a bestseller not only in the United States but in France as well. He convinced the French Tourist Bureau that his books about Madeleine and his drawings of Paris attracted American tourists in droves, to say nothing of the promotion value of his well-known affection for French poodles.

He traveled frequently between New York and Paris— mostly by ship, because he had hypnotized the French Line into transporting himself and his poodles back and forth at no charge.

After a while this humorous blackmail ceased to amuse the French Line, and the time came when Ludwig called to announce his plans for his next crossing and was told that the ship was sold out. There was no available space even for so distinguished a guest as Monsieur Bemelmans.

Ludwig told me what happened next with the delight of a small boy who has just pulled the ears off his sister's stuffed rabbit.

"I called Air France, who of course knew who I was, and told them that while I usually crossed the Atlantic as a guest of the French Line I thought that it would be only fair to give Air France the publicity value of my comments on their impeccable cuisine and ambiance."

Ludwig's face tightened in outrage. "Do you know what their Public Relations officer said?"

I said I didn't.

"He said," Ludwig snorted, "that not only did they not have any first-class seats available, but they couldn't even promise to squeeze me into tourist space for at least six months."

Ludwig shuddered. "I let him wait in silence and then I said, 'thank you very much.'"

The little-boy smirk came back to his face. "When he asked me what for, I said that I was just starting a novel about an airplane that crashed in mid-Atlantic with no survivors and I was wondering what language to have the crew speak."

Harold Guinzburg was an old friend of the Kriendler family who owned and operated the famous "21" Club. He invited me to have lunch there one day with a friend from his OWI days. At some point during the lunch Harold suddenly reminded himself that he had been talking with the family for years about doing a "21" Club cookbook. He sent a message to Mac Kriendler asking him to join us for a discussion after lunch.

We didn't discuss very long. Mac, a handsome man with apparently limitless energy, said it was about time that Harold lit a fire under the project.

Harold had introduced me as both a senior editor at Viking and a man who was a published author and how would Mac like to work with me on the book?

Mac said he would be delighted and we tried to figure out the mechanics of getting a manuscript put together. Mac proposed to dictate the script to his secretary, but he wanted me there while he was doing it. We talked about time and place for this operation and decided on a procedure that had many of the elements of a Harold Lloyd comedy.

The club opened at noon. At 11 every morning Mac had a date in the club's barber shop for a shave, hair trim if necessary, some hot towels and a shoe shine. During this hour his secretary would be there and he would dictate the contents of the cookbook.

Several times a week I would meet Mac and he would start talking about the way the kitchen ran and how their great recipes had been developed. Soon after he started talking, he ordered Bloody Marys for both of us.

When he actually got down to listing the ingredients and procedures for one of their great dishes, he sometimes discovered that he didn't know quite as much as he thought he did about all the details. He would then grab the phone and ask his chef specific questions about how some special dish was prepared. The chef would tell him and Mac would disagree. The arguments were many and frequently impolite. Once in a while the chef would burst into the barbershop to tell Mac he didn't have time to answer all Mac's questions and see that his kitchen was operating as it should at the same time. Mac would calm him down, but a few days later the same scene would be repeated.

When in doubt about something Mac would order us another Bloody Mary to help us decide. During the waiting period for this solvent, he used to tell stories about the family's delicatessen on the lower East Side, how they opened and ran their famous speakeasy during the Prohibition years.

The longest uninterrupted stretch of work we ever got done was in one of the club's chauffeured limousines on a round trip to Lawrenceville School where Mac had to discuss the conduct of one of his nephews.

We never did get the book finished, but I became friendly with members of the family and staff. We used the club for entertaining special authors and visiting publishers, and while I was one of the club's most modest customers I was always greeted and treated warmly and well.

The club did not have many rules, but one that was inviolate was that no columnist or reporter could ever file a story of what somebody was supposed to have said or done during a visit to the club.

As the years went on the club got the reputation of being very exclusive. Mac said they did not seek this distinction. "What are you going to do," he asked, "when a couple from out of town you don't know come in and ask for a table when you have fifteen of your best friends waiting?"

One delightful element of the publishing world at that time was that it was full of baseball fans. At Harcourt I had stolen off to the Polo Grounds with Marion Smith, our chief order clerk, to watch the Giants. Carl Sandburg was a great fan. Robert Frost had been a southpaw pitcher in his youth, and the lovely Marianne Moore was as rabid a Dodger fan as the club ever had. I can remember the shy, penitent look with which she confessed to listening to Dodger games on the radio when she felt she should have been working on her writing. And I'll always remember how she defined poetry as "an imaginary garden with a real toad."

During the eleven-year span of 1947-1957, the *World Series* was played in New York ten times, and on seven occasions two city teams were involved. Maybe nobody referred to the subway series years as a time when diamonds were New York's best friends—but somebody might well have.

For several years, in my official capacity as promotion manager, I booked a table in the dining room of the Waldorf where the Series was being shown on projection TV. Our guests were friendly reviewers, booksellers and authors. We seldom saw all the games, but it was always a fine get together. Some of the regulars were Charles Poore of *The New York Times,* John Hutchens of the *Herald Tribune,* Mark Murphy of *The*

New Yorker, Evaristo Murray of Brentano's, Harvey Breit, the subjunctive lover, and, once in a while, Ken Wilson of the *Reader's Digest.*

Many of the book cities were also baseball cities which had critics and buyers who enjoyed going out to a ball park when business permitted. Philadelphia, Cleveland, Detroit, Chicago, St. Louis—all had teams and players that I enjoyed in the pleasantest of company.

One game that I can remember in almost every detail was the fifth game of the 1956 *World Series* between the Yankees and the Dodgers. I had gone to the game with John and Elaine Steinbeck, and we watched Don Larsen set down twenty-seven Dodgers in succession.

After the last out, John, Elaine and I hugged each other, reveling in the excitement of having watched a sports masterpiece—the first no-hitter in *World Series* history and the first perfect *World Series* game in history.

In 1957 we were living in a big, old pre-Revolutionary house just off South Mountain Road in Rockland County. One Sunday morning in late spring while Emily was visiting a friend in Connecticut and my sister Kay was spending the weekend at our house, Arthur Miller called to say that he and the kids would like to come out and cook hotdogs in our backyard if it was all right with us.

It was a lot more that all right. Arthur and I hadn't spent too much time together, but we had found a good deal of pleasant common ground. At one lunch I remember we traded memories of New York in the Depression years. We got right down to which newspaper we folded up to stuff in our shoes before we could spare the money to have them half-soled. Later on, during a visit to his workroom in the East Side apartment, I asked him how the new play was coming. He pointed to a ten-inch pile of manuscript and said he had 1200 pages of it done.

I asked how many pages there would be in the final version.

"About a hundred and twenty-five," he said.

Viking had just published an edition of his collected plays for which he had written a fifty-page introduction which I found to be the most revealing and stimulating essay I had ever read on the art and craft of the playwright.

Just as I was finishing giving Arthur directions on how to get to our house, our son Nick wandered into the room. Nick was seventeen and in another year was to follow his older brother to college. He asked who was coming out and I told him one of our authors.

"Which one?" Nick asked.

"Arthur Miller."

"Oh yes, he's, let's see, he wrote *Death of a Salesman.*"

"Right," I said, "he's bringing his kids."

Nick said, "And he's married to..." His voice changed as if he had been hit by an electric shock. "He's married to Marilyn Monroe. Is she coming?"

"I'm not sure," I said.

Nick grabbed for the phone. "I'm going to call some friends..."

I cut him short. "You are going to do no such thing. That's just what they're coming out here to avoid."

At this point Nick took one of the most surprising and unpredictable actions of his life. He got out the vacuum cleaner and started cleaning house. My sister had the same kind of impulse and made for the bathroom to see if it was ready for visitors.

Our visitors arrived about noon in a Ford convertible. My first impression was that Arthur had three children with him. He got out first and stood tall beside the car as Jane and Bobby jumped out followed by an attractive older child wearing a bandanna around her hair, a man's shirt with rolled-up sleeves with the shirttails tied at her waist and corduroy slacks. Suddenly I realized that it wasn't a third child, it was Marilyn. She was carrying a picnic basket.

We went in to the living room and sat down. Looking at the real Marilyn instead of a picture of her was fascinating and moving. She looked at us with an almost eager expectancy—as though she hoped she'd like us.

She was entirely without pose, artifice or make-up. Her hair, even with the kerchief, was windblown. Seated beside me on the couch with the tentative look leaving her brown eyes, her lightly freckled face glowing, she was every man's memory of the girl he had fallen in love with when he was sixteen.

It was a relaxed, easy-going gathering from the beginning. If there was a hint of tension it was between Jane, Bobby and Marilyn. She and Arthur had been married the previous June, so it was only natural that his children had some adjusting to do.

We all went out to the little wild area behind the house and gathered wood for our fire. Arthur and I decided to sit and talk and let the others do the work.

Then it was time to cook and eat and afterwards Nick brought out some of the family's baseball equipment and he and Bobby and

Jane began to toss the softball around. This seemed like fun so I suggested that we drive down the road to Jack Masters' place where there was lawn enough to have a little family game of softball.

Everyone thought that was a fine idea so I called Jack to see if he and Barbara were both available and agreeable. They were.

Family softball games are enjoyable in inverse ratio to how well they are played. We had a kind of combination three-O-cat and teams. But the formal organization wasn't important. It was a lovely afternoon. All of us played every position. There was much racing and chasing, the catching of balls and the dropping of balls, the hitting of pitches and the missing of pitches.

After a while, the game developed a dimension that hadn't been part of any ball game I'd ever heard of. When Marilyn was playing first base no runner ever even ran to second base—much less tried to steal it. Same thing when she played second and third. We tried and failed to enforce a rule that there could be only one base runner on a base at a time. We considered asking her to be the catcher, but decided that was a terrible idea because every hit would be a home run. Arthur was a good player, but he managed to drop his share of balls and throw ten feet over the catcher's head without being ostentatious about it.

Marilyn was a completely inexperienced player, but her enthusiasm more than made up for her mistakes. The first two or three times she was at bat she struck out, but the high point of the game, for everyone, came when my sister Kay pitched a ball over the middle of home plate and Marilyn with a mighty swing drove the ball over the head of my son Nick, who was naturally playing as close to her as he could, into the neighbor's driveway for a home run. We all cheered as Marilyn romped around the bases.

After we'd had enough softball, Jack and Barbara asked us into the house for tea. Marilyn was bubbling. She said she had been to a few baseball games but her ex-husband Joe (DiMaggio) had never explained what all the running around everybody was doing was for.

She looked around at all of us and said, with an incandescent smile, "I never knew how much fun baseball could be."

My wife Emily had come home in time to read the note I had left on the back door and came to the game, but not in time to see

Marilyn's home run. Emily is one of the world's great movie fans and I could tell by the way she looked at Marilyn that she found her enormously appealing. My son Chris, who was away at college, is as much a baseball fan as his mother is a movie fan. He has never forgiven me for letting this particular game happen without him.

When the Millers got in their car to start back to the city Marilyn snuggled into the corner of the back seat and then Jane and Bobby got to arguing about who was to sit in the front seat with their father. I've forgotten who won.

The next time we saw Arthur and Marilyn was at a dinner at Pat Covici's apartment in New York. The guests were old friends of the Millers and there was some good natured discussion of how late they would be. Pat said he had called Arthur and reminded him that he and Marilyn were expected at 7 p.m. and they'd better be on time.

At five minutes past the hour the doorbell rang. When Pat opened the door everyone was astounded. Arthur and Marilyn stood there, on time and smiling. Marilyn was carrying a large paper bag. She gave Pat her most winning smile and said that if she'd stayed home to finish dressing she would have been late so she brought her things with her and would finish getting ready in Mrs. Covici's room. Forty- five minutes later we sat down to dinner.

Most of the conversation at dinner centered around Judaic studies. Marilyn had recently begun studies in this field, and I think two of the men she had been working with were at the table. I don't know what kind of student she was or how far her studies took her. She didn't talk very much during the discussion, but when her clear, soft voice sounded and she looked at Arthur you knew where she hoped her studies would lead.

In September of 1957 Viking published *On The Road* by Jack Kerouac. A review in *The New York Times* by Gilbert Millstein called it a major novel and said its publication was an "...historic occasion insofar as the exposure of an authentic work of art is of any great moment."

Most critics, however, disagreed with Millstein's opinion, in spite of which the book became an immediate sensation. More than that, Jack Kerouac became accepted as the seer of the "beat" generation just as Hemingway had become the prophet of the generation called "lost."

I have been pretty deeply identified with the publication of this book mostly because I was a kind of point man on its tortured path from manuscript to book.

Jack told several stories about how he came to write it. In explaining the sequence of its composition I'm inclined to go with the account in Tom Clarke's fine biography. Clarke went into the whole scene in great detail and I disagree with him on only a few points.

Apparently Jack had finished one version of the book in 1947 which he abandoned—but never completely. Four years later in Florida, he told me, his wife said she was sick of his sitting around telling stories about his adventures and the people he adventured with and why didn't he sit down and write it out.

This is exactly what Jack did. He was an expert typist, but it always interrupted his flow of words to have to stop and put in a new piece of paper. He solved this problem by gluing together sheets of onionskin drawing paper and part of a roll of teletype paper into a single sheet 100 yards in length. At least that's what Jack said. I never measured it. He hung the roll so that the paper would feed into his typewriter and out to lie in a heap on the floor. He worked for six weeks and poured out his prose in one unparagraphed, single spaced torrent of 150,000 words.

Jack submitted the book to Harcourt, Brace with a characteristic gesture. He set Bob Giroux, his editor, at one end of the main office hallway, walked to the other end and unrolled the manuscript towards Bob's feet with the motion of a bowler. Bob's first reaction was to ask how the hell a printer could work from a manuscript like that. The query enraged Kerouac and he stormed out of the office without giving Bob a chance to read a word of it.

At that point Phyllis Jackson at MCA became Jack's agent and sent the scroll of *On The Road* and several other manuscripts to Malcolm Cowley, whose interest and confidence in Jack's writing future had never weakened. Malcolm gave me the manuscript to read and I was almost blown away by it. Nearly everything that can be said about the book has been said. By the time I had finished my reading of it I could make up no sentences to define the way I felt about it. The closest I can come to it now is to quote an observation of Emerson that I underlined in Mark Van Doren's wonderful introduction to the Viking Portable Emerson:

"...flows like a river—so unconsidered, so humorous, so pathetic, such justice done to all the parts. It is a true substantiation—the fact converted into speech all warm and colored and alive, as it fell out."

I gave the manuscript to Helen Taylor to read and she felt much as I did. We then talked to Malcolm about ways and means to get Viking to publish this book. The first thing, we decided, was to have it retyped on standard sheets so we could put the scroll away for posterity. When this was done we had Pat Covici read it. It was a little too wild and careless to appeal to Pat, but he said he would support us when decision time came.

I'm not sure exactly how long we had the book in work at Viking, but it must have been the better part of two years. I never did any work on textual changes—that was done by Malcolm and Helen. Our feeling was that the text should have some paragraphing and that different tellings of the same happenings be combined. But what took the most time was the discussion of whether the book should be presented as non-fiction, or, after all names had been changed, as fiction.

The Viking lawyers felt that because there was so much use of illegal substances and damage and theft of other people's cars that all the names should be changed and the book labeled as fiction. The lawyers were certain that if we published the book as non-fiction that legal action would be taken against most of the characters in the book.

During these months Jack was out of touch for long periods of time and there was no way for us to reach him. Finally, in New York, Malcolm and I did have a chance to sit down with him and discuss the whole matter of publication. As gently as we could, we put it to him that if he wanted to see Viking publish the book he had to go along with the fiction approach and change the names. He was not pleased by this condition, no author would be, but he finally agreed, made the changes and went on the road again. The editorial board finally accepted it.

He came back to New York to do some promotion work with me at publication time and he did it very well. We spent a good deal of time in downtown music bars, and the day the Millstein review appeared in *The New York Times* I showed up at his current pad with a couple of bottles of champagne.

I didn't hang out much with Jack and his friends. After all, I was in my late forties and clearly of another generation. But I found that the beat generation had many qualities that I felt very good about. Most of them celebrated each other's creativity and were gentle and generous with their companions. Their public behavior was often unacceptable to their elders as, I'm sure, ours was to them. Our generation had already produced enough atomic and hydrogen bombs to obliterate the human race several times over and it must have seemed quite possible that this was just what might happen. Perhaps they felt they deserved a better future than extinction.

Jack's next book was *Dharma Bums*. It was a different, more conventional book than the Road and one I liked very much. I worked with Jack on the text and we got along well. When we were finished he gave me the scroll of *On The Road* as a mark of his friendship. I kept it for several years and finally at the invitation of Fred Adams gave it to the Morgan Library for their celebrated manuscript collection.

About a month after the library had finished their restoration and preservation work on it Sterling Lord, Jack's last literary agent, called me to say that Jack was very sick and very broke and needed the manuscript back to sell. The Morgan Library released the manuscript to Lord and that's the last I heard of it.

I never saw Jack after the publication of *Dharma Bums.* Those who loved him were helpless in the face of his compulsion to destroy his talent and himself. He died in October 1969 and according to an essay of his published in various newspapers just before his death, he was "an inconsolable orphan...all bespotted and gloomed-up in the nightsoil of poor body and soul."

31

In the last week of September 1957 New York City booksellers were mobbed by customers wanting to buy copies of Stendahl's *The Red and the Black*. Liveright sold out their stock of the hardcover edition, Random House shipped all their copies of the Modern Library edition of this classic French novel, originally published in 1830, and in one day Brentano's Bookstore sold more copies than had been sold in the author's lifetime.

All this was caused by a new CBS half-hour TV show called *Sunrise Semester* which was aired at 6:30 a.m., featuring an intense young New York University professor named Floyd Zulli.

Sunrise Semester was not the first course in literature to be televised, but it was the first to have such impact. Floyd was in love with the classics and spoke of them with irresistible enthusiasm and excitement—not as a critic but as a reader. His presentation of Stendahl's masterpiece convinced many thousands of people that reading the book was an absorbing experience that they couldn't possibly miss.

One of his colleagues at NYU described a Zulli performance: "I remember there was one scene in the book in which Zulli played about eight parts while just sitting in a chair."

Of course the plot of *The Red and the Black* was unusual for its time. The main character is a power-hungry opportunist—a seducer of women and a betrayer of employers. If this sounds like the TV hits *Dallas* and *Dynasty* it may be just coincidence. There's one plot device in Stendhal's book that would have made a bang-up ending to one of those series.

In *The Red and the Black,* Julien Sorel, our despicable hero, is guillotined for shooting his mistress because she has revealed the true nature of his character to the father of his pregnant girl friend. Julien's body is taken to a cave in the mountains where the girl friend buries his head with her own hands. Later she decorates the cave with Italian marble.

Floyd was a generous man, he would have forgiven me for having a little fun with the novel termed by one critic "...one of the most polished and refined artistic stones in the literary crown of European literature." Floyd would have agreed with this verdict, but he certainly wouldn't have written about it that way.

Floyd wrote a book for me called *The Joy of Reading* which never got the audience it deserved, possibly because it did not have an ardent TV spokesman with his genius for bringing books alive to potential readers. Floyd won four New York *Emmy* awards, including one for the outstanding television personality of 1957-58.

In *The Prelude* Wordsworth wrote: "What we have loved, others will love and we may teach them how." Floyd Zulli accomplished this by making us feel that he was handing out maps to not-so-buried treasures in the world of reading that would enrich us for the rest of our lives.

The startling success of the Zulli program suggested the exciting potential of television to create new readers for all kinds of books.

During the Viking years I was paid fairly and got regular raises without having to ask, but I could see two sons on their way to college so I kept on writing.

In 1953 Doubleday published a satire called *The Half-Open Road,* A Handy Guide to Chaos on the Highway. It got fine reviews all over the place mostly, I concluded later, due to the marvelous illustrations by George Price. Quite a few people thought the book was trenchant, wicked and hilarious—just as it was supposed to be. But its sales, or rather its lack of sales, proved the truth of a remark by George Abbot, who said, "Satire is what closes on Saturday."

A year later Bill Sloane published my first novel *The Green Place* and I was referred to as a writer to watch. I hope not too many people took this advice because I didn't publish another novel for twenty-five years.

In the summer of 1954 I wrote a play. It had a deeply felt theme, offset, I hoped, by some pretty antic goings on. It was finally produced off-Broadway as a showcase production, but that's as far as it got.

In 1956 though, Viking published a book of mine called *The Boys and Their Mother.* I wrote this as a result of taking the advice I often gave young writers, to the effect that they should write about things they know and feel deeply about. The reviews of this book were embarrassingly good and it made *The New York Times* best-seller list. There was another week when there was so much good news about the book in the offing that it was hard to go to sleep.

Friends at the Book-of-the-Month Club told me they were pretty sure the judges were going to take it. Another friend at *Reader's*

Digest called to say that he thought the *Digest* was going to take it, too. Harold Guinzburg had a producer friend who thought it would make an appealing musical comedy. None of these things happened, but it was quite a week and I didn't spend any of the money.

I suppose writing was both my insulation from reality and my method of coming to terms with it. Whichever it was, the result made it possible for me to get along well with other writers because I shared their vanity and vulnerability. I had been close to several important writers but I had never felt competitive. I knew I was never going to be an important writer, but that wasn't the point. I have never published a line I am ashamed of, and I've never published a line that I don't think somehow could have been better. To put it at its simplest, I guess the commitment was to a skill I could hope to improve as long as I lived.

This commitment was strong enough to be a major factor in a career change that I made in 1958. John Tebbel, a publishing name I knew, but a man I didn't, called and invited me to have lunch with him to discuss a new graduate program at New York University.

Jack was a veteran newspaperman, book editor and author of—among other books—the acclaimed *George Washington's America.* At the time of our lunch he was chairman of the New York University Journalism Department.

His news was that NYU had been given an endowment to establish a graduate school of book publishing. The University would offer a two-semester Master's degree from the Department of Education. Jack had been transferred from the Journalism Department to become director of the new institute. It was a tremendously exciting program. There had never been a concentrated two-semester course of study for young people who had decided upon a career in book publishing. He had discussed the program with many book publishers. They were firmly behind the new program and offered all the cooperation Jack would need.

The staff would consist of Jack, an assistant director, and an executive secretary. The student body, at least at the beginning, would be limited to thirty. These students would spend their mornings as interns in cooperating publishing houses, their afternoons at the Institute listening to lectures from specialists in all phases of publishing and working on related hands-on projects of their own, and at night they would take required courses needed to qualify for their advanced degree.

The job of the assistant director would be to design and run the publishing workshops and arrange for the visiting experts. Jack said he had approached my brother Peter in the matter of the assistant directorship but Peter, who was at that time Assistant Managing Director of the Book Publishers Council, felt that it was not the right time for him to make a move and suggested that Jack ask me.

Peter's first novel had just been published and he was deeply involved in anti-censorship actions, the Freedom to Read Committee, and the APBC International Trade Committee.

"The job carries an appointment as full professor," Jack said. "Are you interested?"

I asked what a full professor was paid. Jack told me and I was interested. I'm not at all sure that Jack told me that I would be working the academic year if I took the job or whether I just assumed it. In any event this factor had a great deal to do with my decision to accept the offer.

I was quite used to living a dual life—as writer and publisher—and teaching out of almost twenty-five years of experience in all the facets of book publishing seemed very appropriate and would combine well with the writing plans I had made. After a week of on-the-one-hand-this and on-the- other-hand-that, I took the job.

Leaving Viking was one of the most painful experiences of my life. It was a closely knit organization of dedicated people with whom I had shared many successes and inevitable failures. We cared about our books, we cared about our authors, and we cared about each other.

I was given a farewell office party that almost demolished me, but at least my decision was one they could understand. I left the lovely May Massee's office and hurried to the men's room to dry my face, for she had said, "Send us your students and that will mean we never lost you at all."

From the very beginning the Institute was all that I had hoped for and more. Jack had made a deal with the University to take the program off campus so, after a lot of looking around, we found some ideal space at 131 Madison Avenue. It was no more than one huge showroom, and all we did was add a low stage at the window end and two narrow partitions to mark the difference between the classroom and the office.

As soon as we began to make a budget for the furniture we would need, I remembered a remark a visiting English publisher had made upon leaving the office-warming party of William Sloane Associates. Jonathan Cape had said, "This firm is bound to fail; it doesn't know the price of a second-hand typewriter."

Jack's secretary in the journalism department, Jemison Hammond—former wife of Columbia Records' John Hammond—had come with him to the Institute and Jack and Jemmy and I furnished the place with second-hand typewriters, chairs, desks, rugs and tables. I think the only thing we bought new was a coffee maker.

As soon as we had an official address and stationery, the University promotion people went to work to get us applications. They sent posters out to colleges and universities across the country, and Jack and I began to make plans for just what we were going to do and how we were going to do it. We agreed that we were not going to run a trade school, that taking our course would not be immediately rewarded with a job. And even if it did, it would probably be the same job that the student would have gotten without taking the course. But, as the student's skills and career commitment became apparent the employer would bring him or her along very quickly into better positions.

All this happened not too long after Yale University had gone on the college system and I had read a story about a note on the bulletin board of one of the new colleges that read, "ONLY UPPER CLASSMEN ARE PERMITTED TO WALK ACROSS THE LAWN. (This tradition goes into effect today.)"

Jack and I decided that, being an institution of higher learning, we would develop traditions of our own the same way. I think the first tradition was that the students had to dress formally each morning for work at a publisher's office. It could be filing invoices, emptying wastebaskets, going out for coffee and sandwiches, collating manuscripts, anything—no matter how menial. The publisher was paying the student's tuition and if the student couldn't accept the chore work it was just too bad. If the student quit the apprenticeship he or she quit the Institute simultaneously. Nobody did.

Jack had the course work that the NYU Department of Education required all organized. It was up to me to organize the workshops. I had no formal background in education theory and practice and spent many confusing and frustrating hours trying to figure out the exact format that would accomplish what we wanted for our students. I had spoken at enough colleges around the country to get the feeling that the more college students were treated like grown-ups the more they behaved like grown-ups.

Somehow I remembered the format that Jack Masters had told me about that was used by the British War College. Young officers who attended were divided into groups of six which were called syndicates. (Apparently the British were not acquainted with Mafia gangs using the same name.) Each syndicate was given an identical problem in military logistics of some kind. The group went to work and arrived at a solution. At this point the group leader—which changed with every new problem—joined the leaders of the other groups and presented his group's solution for examination, comment and debate by the whole class.

I thought this seemed like a good format for my future publishers. It may not have been ideal, but it certainly worked.

Applications began to arrive in every mail. We ended up with more than 300 from Maine to Oregon, Miami to San Diego and points in between. Some we could accept on the basis of their application and many could be denied for what their application revealed. Naturally, the more numerous the applications the harder the selection process became. We finally realized that in some cases we would want personal interviews before making a decision. It might amount to a financial hardship, but we felt we needed it to make a fair choice.

So the class assembled and we were delighted with them. The curriculum was a beast, but they were motivated over their heads and there were no real complaints. The publishing industry furnished lecturers and consultants in all aspects of publishing. Then I'd assign projects for the groups to work on in the area covered by the speaker of the day before. I believe we covered all the major technical areas of expertise that a real knowledge of book publishing demands: design, paper, printing, binding, editing, promotion, advertising, sales and the basics of publishing costs and their control. Book selection began to be discussed when I changed the groups into imaginary publishing houses; made them select books, write basic copy about them, decide on advertising campaigns and special sales coverages.

We had visits from the most eminent lawyers in the publishing field, copyright experts and censorship experts. It was a wonderful, busy time.

During the summer Harold McGraw had called me to ask if I would consider becoming an advisor to the McGraw-Hill trade department. The job required one morning a week at their editorial meeting, and consulting on any manuscripts on which my opinion would be of value. I thought that was a fine idea. I could be spared from the Institute during the morning.

One of the first of the readings I did for McGraw-Hill was a manuscript called *Endurance* by Alfred Lansing. It was the story of the British explorer Sir Ernest Shackleton's last and most unbelievably heroic polar expedition. The book was stunningly good, so good in fact that a shadow of suspicion crossed my mind. I wrote a rave opinion of the work, forecast book-club selection and bestsellerdom. But I suggested that one of the editors compare it with other works on or by the great man.

A week or so later my phone at the Institute rang and a man's voice said, "I hear you think I'm a plagiarist. I'm Al Lansing and I really did write the book."

I've forgotten what I replied, but the next day I took Al to lunch and we had a fine time. He was one of the writers recruited by *Time-Life Books* to write some of their books, but the Shackleton he had written out of admiration and excitement. The book was taken by the Book-of-the-Month Club and did get on, and stay on, the bestseller lists. Al and I became friends and saw each other occasionally for years.

I didn't spend much time with the McGraw-Hill people, but I did become more sensitive to some of the new responsibilities of management, especially in the terms of employee medical benefits. This led me to consider the position of the author in relationship to insurance and medical cost protection. I wondered if there wasn't some way that an author's royalty money, owed by the publisher, could be used for health and life insurance for the author before it was paid to the author so it wouldn't be taxable. I talked with a man from the Jameison Insurance Group and he became interested in the idea.

After a good deal of study and consultation the lawyers and the insurance specialists worked out a trial contract which made the author an employee of the publisher under specified conditions and with specified tasks that qualified the author for the company medical coverage at a cost far below what the same coverage would cost a self-employed person.

The IRS man we talked to said it looked all right to his people, but warned that final approval could not be given in advance of a legal test case. Gay Talese wrote a little story about the new contract for *The New York Times* and I was told that McGraw-Hill used the contract once, but I am not aware that the experiment changed the course of book publishing contracts. I was disappointed and so was the insurance company that financed the research.

The young men and women of the Institute's first class never ceased surprising us with their dedication, effort and enthusiasm. They worked with imagination and creativity. And they worked hard. So hard in fact that Jack and I frequently had to invent a pretext for having a party. Our students really didn't have either the time or the money to enjoy New York nightlife and after a few weeks of 16-hour work days they would get tired and tense.

Jack and I would take the class's stress temperature and when it got too high we would plan a relaxing social event. Usually we'd look in an almanac and see whose birthday would be appropriate—or entirely inappropriate, it didn't really matter— close the workshops early, set up a wine and beer bar, open up boxes of crackers and let nature take its course.

Sometimes we would ask well-known figures from the book publishing world to attend our urban clambakes. We had many distinguished guests, but the visit of Alfred Knopf was probably the best remembered. He was such an eminent and admired figure that the students reacted almost with awe. The only advance briefing I had done was to remind them that the K in his name was not silent.

Another memorable visit was from William Jovanovich, the dynamic new president of Harcourt, Brace and Company. He spoke passionately about the responsibilities of good publishing. Bill had risen to his current rank through re-vitalizing the HB text departments. He closed his remarks by saying that his trade department was always in an uproar. It acted, Bill said, like a man who had determined to have a baby in one month by the process of impregnating nine women.

At some point in the previous ten years I had taken up playing the guitar and practicing singing some of the Burl Ives folk songs that I loved. During the annual American booksellers conventions, which greatly resembled house parties at which hosts and guests almost drowned in the rivers of publishers' hospitality, I took to singing these songs late at night to the most uncritical audiences an amateur performer ever had. I even made up new words to one of the best known ballad tunes.

At one time the format of the National Book Awards included a pre-announcement lunch for all the visiting out-of-town critics. Somebody from the awards committee called me and asked if I felt like writing a song especially for this occasion. I felt so complimented that I said I would.

I have no idea what anybody expected in the way of a song, but the more I thought about this challenge, the more tempted I was to write a song from an author's standpoint. It was irresistible. In time, the following song became known as "The Author's Song." It was sung to the great old English ballad "Sam Hall." Verse by verse it follows the content of the original which was sung by a man on the gallows who wanted the spectators to know who he was and what he thought of the proceedings. In its first performance I mentioned that my words were set to a famous folk song, and its first verse was the same in my version. I told the critics that it was going to be a song that an author sang to his publishers and began it by reminding them what his name was because he was sure they had forgotten it.

Oh my name it is Sam Hall, is Sam Hall
Oh my name it is Sam Hall, is Sam Hall
Oh my name it is Sam Hall
And I hate you one and all
Yes I hate you one and all
Damn your eyes.

Oh I wrote a book you said, yes you said,
Oh I wrote a book you said, yes you said,
Oh I wrote a book you said
And you left it there for dead,
Yes you left it there for dead
Damn your eyes.

Oh my agent came to town, came to town
Oh my agent came to town, came to town
Oh my agent came to town
Set his price
But he came down
Oh he came way down
Damn his eyes.

Oh the editor came too, he came too
Oh the editor came too, he came too
Oh the editor came too
With his little pencil blue
Oh that little pencil blue
Damn his eyes.

The salesmen went to sell, went to sell,
The salesmen went to sell, went to sell,
The salesmen went to sell,
Where they went they wouldn't tell,
But I'll see them in hell,
Damn their eyes.

I saw Michener on the list, on the list
I saw Michener on the list, on the list
I saw Michener on the list

177

And I wished to God he'd missed
If he'd only missed just once
Damn his eyes.

On publication day, on the day
On publication day, on the day
On publication day what did the critics have to say?

(silence)

That's what the critics had to say
Damn their eyes.
So it's off to Marboro, Marboro,
So it's off to Marboro, Marboro,
So it's off to Marboro*
And you're glad to see me go,
Yes, you're glad to see me go,
Damn your eyes.

* Marboro was the name of a chain of bookstores that dealt primarily with stocks of books the publisher couldn't sell.

So there was usually some kind of singing going on at the parties either by very mixed voices or from one of the student's radios.

Jack and Jemmy and I didn't get mixed up with the students' private lives. They were adults and deserved to be left alone to live their New York lives the way they saw fit. Once in a while, but very rarely, we were asked for help of one kind or another.

The workshop syndicate system was working out well. It seemed to us that the members of the class were learning how to keep their individual competitive drives from damaging the group effort.

Jack's course in the history of publishing was a major event and visiting lecturers always commented on both the attention they were accorded and the quality of the questions that were raised.

We were visited by a group of higher education monitors

and given a heartening appraisal of what we appeared to be accomplishing.

One day, late that fall, I stood in the ashes of our house looking up through blackened rafters at a cold November sky.

The insurance inspector standing beside me said, "Jesus, didn't they used to build them." The house had been there before the Hessians sailed up the Hudson to Haverstraw.

Three days before, Emily and I had stopped at a friend's house for cocktails on our way back from the station. Another friend called to say there was a fire up the road and it might be our house. It was, and by the time we got there it was too far gone to hope to save anything. The firemen had done the best they could. There were no hydrants and it was a long way to the little neighboring pond.

The police told us that the fire had been started by a retarded youth from a facility not too far away, who had found the house open and came in to cook himself something to eat. He had mishandled the gas stove, the kitchen curtains had caught fire and in almost no time the house was beyond rescue. The body of Mrs. Goat, our gray and white tiger cat, had been found by one of the firemen.

I stood waiting for shock or pain to hit, but all I felt was numb. We spent the night with Bill and Julie Sloane and when the rubble had cooled we searched for small things that were precious to us. All the pictures were gone, some looter had found where the silver had been kept and had stolen a set of little spoons that had belonged to Emily's grandmother.

Then the neighbors began to arrive. With food, clothes, wanting to know what they could do. The Conklin family who had been growing apples up the road from us for 300 years sent us a message that they had an unused wing of their house and we could move in any time we felt like it.

The next night the thermometer dropped to the teens and the rubble froze. I could hardly bear to face the book shelves and book cases. I suppose there were a thousand or more books that we had cherished and moved from house to house over the years. Favorites from our childhood, inscribed copies, first editions, fine bindings, all were scorched or charred to one degree or another.

My collection of Frost's volumes of poetry had been gutted by fire and ice. It took two days to select the books that could be kept. I stacked these beside the remnants of our collection of recordings. Then I realized that I had to get rid of the books that were damaged beyond further use. Somehow it didn't occur to me to leave them there and let them be buried by the inevitable bulldozer.

I borrowed a comic little truck—half pick-up and half Ford sedan—loaded the mutilated books and set off for the town dump. The sanitary landfill was slippery with mud and I made slow progress across the slimy wasteland. I backed into the most remote corner of the lot and threw books out— one by one—without looking to see where they fell. Then I drove back to the main road, found a bar and stayed there for a long time.

The second semester of the Institute was even better than the first. The students got leaner and smarter and more exciting to be with. However, as the semester neared its final weeks I began to understand from my contacts at the University that I had misunderstood the terms of my employment. I was supposed to work a twelve month year, not a nine month year. I was disturbed by this possibility because working the academic year had been one of the major factors in my leaving Viking to do more writing of my own. I had made definite plans to spend several weeks in England with Emily that summer, a trip we had long been looking forward to. I wanted to explore the possibilities of doing a non-fiction book cast as the biography of a castle—Dover, perhaps, Ludlow or Kenilworth.

Before I even had a chance to discuss the problem with Jack I was asked if I would consider returning to publishing. The inquiry came from Carol Brandt one of the most attractive and influential literary agents in New York.

Carol and I had lunch and she told me that the David McKay Company was looking for an editor-in-chief to expand their publishing range.

I knew little about the firm except that Ken Rawson, the owner, and his wife Eleanor had breathed new life into an old firm, and had been joined by two men that I knew well and admired: Quentin Bossi was sales manager and one of the finest men I had ever met: Ted Mills, a close friend from prep school days, was in charge of the associated U.S. interests of Longmans, Green. Ken Rawson was a tough, determined man who had been at the South Pole with

Admiral Byrd and had earned a Navy Cross during World War II. His wife Eleanor was a smart, attractive woman with a remarkable editorial flair that brought many bestsellers to the firm. It was an interesting situation and one, I told Carol Brandt, I would like to explore.

After a long meeting with the Rawsons, Mills and Bossi, I was offered a vice-presidency and the position of editor-in-chief. The immediate financial arrangement was generous, and there would be a profit-sharing deal to follow. In addition, Mrs. Brandt said she had an interesting author with a fine book for me immediately and there would be more to come.

I had one more talk with Rawson, told him of my commitment to our trip to England, and Ken told me to go ahead with my plans. Further, he said, if I wanted to see some of the English publishers while I was in London I could charge off some of my expenses to the firm.

The offer was irresistible. I hated to leave Jack and the Institute but, in a way, he understood some of my reasons if not all of them.

Soon after I joined McKay I met with Carol Brandt to hear about the author and the manuscript she wanted me to consider. The meeting led to my friendship with one of the most enjoyable and fascinating men I have ever known.

Gene Markey was best known as the Hollywood producer who had been married in turn, to Joan Bennett, Hedy Lamarr, and Myrna Loy. Until my conversation with Carol I didn't know he had written several novels and screen plays as well as a favorably received recent historical novel about Kentucky.

During our talk Carol referred to him several times as the Admiral. When I asked her, somewhat rudely, what he was admiral of, she told me that he had recently been retired from the United States Navy with the rank of Rear Admiral. Later on I looked up his military record and was much impressed. Gene had been an infantry lieutenant in World War I, joined the Naval Reserve in 1920. He was called to active duty after Pearl Harbor and was awarded a Bronze Star for leading a reconnaissance mission in the Solomon Islands in 1942. He had also received the Legion of Merit and France's Legion of Honor.

When I asked Carol where his interest in Kentucky had come from she told me that in 1952 he had married Lucille Wright the owner of Calumet Farm. I was never much of a follower of thoroughbred racing, but I knew that Calumet Farm had won more Kentucky Derbys and more racing Triple Crowns in recent years than any other thoroughbred racing establishment.

Carol was fond of Gene and Lucille and said that I would be too. She was right.

Gene's book was called *That Far Paradise* and I liked it very much. The adventure romance was about the dangerous trip a family made from their ancestral home in Virginia to make a new home in Kentucky after the Revolutionary War. It was thoroughly researched, vividly written and all in all a very rewarding reading experience.

As soon as I had read it, and described it in a McKay editorial meeting, I called Carol and said that we wanted to publish it. I told her I did have a few details I wanted to talk over with the author—nothing major—and wondered how soon and where I could meet him for discussion.

Carol told me that Gene and Lucille were in Italy and wouldn't be available for a month. I looked at my calendar and told her that in a month Emily and I would be in England. A few days later she called back and reported that the Markey's planned to fly to London, take a suite at Claridge's and would be happy to see me there at my convenience.

I had never heard of an editor, even an in-chief editor, being treated quite this lavishly but the arrangement sounded great to Emily and me. Through the good offices of a friend who was a member of The Players in New York, I was accepted as an overseas member of the Chelsea Arts Club in London and that is where I planned to stay.

The Chelsea Arts Club had been founded in 1891 by James Whistler and his friends and now stands on the Sloane Stanley Estate. The club house was once two eighteenth century cottages with a spacious garden. The tiny guest rooms were comfortable and astonishingly inexpensive, the food exceptionally good and the members friendly and welcoming.

I had never been the guest of a guest at Claridge's, but it didn't take long for me to understand how it had earned its fame as one of the most select hotels in any world capital.

Gene and I worked five or six hours over a two-day period. We agreed on a few minor changes and not on others. He was pleasant, warm, and humorous but I was always conscious of his basic intensity and strength.

Lucille met us on arrival and then left to visit a friend in the country who had some thoroughbreds she wanted her to see. Emily spent time trying to find china in a pattern that she knew my mother loved.

The second night, to celebrate finishing the editorial work on the book, Gene took Emily and me out for a special dinner. I can't remember the meal dish by dish, all unbelievably good, but I will never forget the dessert. The waiter placed lovely, long stemmed crystal goblets in front of us, each containing a beautifully ripe, cored and peeled pear. After presenting a bottle of Charles Heidsick champagne for Gene's approval, the waiter filled our goblets almost to the rim.

We talked over a glass of brandy that was older than Napoleon, agreed on the next steps for the manuscript and made a date to see each other in New York when Gene had completed the re-working of the manuscript that we had agreed upon.

The resident London representative of McKay had written notes to several London publishers informing them that the new editor-in-chief of McKay would be in London for a while and would be calling to make an appointment. The note must have mentioned the Chelsea Arts Club because I received invitations by phone and mail at that address and was greatly complimented by my cordial reception.

I don't remember all the meetings but several were so remarkably pleasant that the memory of them has stayed fresh in my mind.

William (not yet Sir William) Collins asked us for lunch at his home on St. James Square. Emily and I were so pleased by the invitation that we brought a dozen red roses to our hostess. Number 14 St. James Square was an exquisite Queen Anne house and the Collins were the warmest of hosts. Mrs. Collins was a rose enthusiast and it happened that we had picked out a bouquet of one of her favorite varieties. It was a lovely visit and Emily was touched by two postcards that Mrs. Collins sent her later from a country estate in Kent. The first saying the roses had withstood the train trip very well, and the second describing how beautiful the roses looked on the table in the library.

Roger Maitchell, of Hamish Hamilton invited us for tea at his flat in The Albany, one of the most famous apartment dwellings in London. Behind the main residence, Roger told us, there were individual small townhouses facing a central garden. Previous tenants in these accommodations were Disraeli, Gladstone, Asquith, Lloyd George and other notable personages.

The thing I remembered most clearly about Lloyd George was that he was reputed to have been an implacable foe of Winston Churchill. I asked Roger if this was so.

Roger said it most certainly was. "Once he said that Winston would use his mother's skin to make a drum to beat his own praises on."

London publishing lunches were very much like those I was accustomed to in New York—long and leisurely. I met Mark Longman who was an old friend of my colleague Ted Mills at McKay; Jonathan Cape was the most delightful of companions; Michael Joseph was Jack Masters' UK publisher so we had much to talk about. All in all the London days were relaxed and rewarding without exception. But we were eager to get out of the city.

Emily and I hired a VW and went sight-seeing and castle hunting. We stayed some days in Ludlow, walked the hills that Houseman had walked and read the poems of the great scholar in his role as a country boy mourning the passing of youth and love. We walked the walls of Chester and York and what was left of Kenilworth. We loved every minute of it.

It took a great deal of concentration to learn to drive on the left hand side of the road—especially in the roundabouts where everything seemed to be going in the wrong direction. Nothing about driving could be left to the reflexes. One day we were going up a narrow, unpaved road to a pub we had heard about and over the top of the hill coming right at us was a Rover. My instincts made me pull over to my right, just as the Englishman driving the Rover pulled his car to the left. We had both put on our brakes and all that happened was that our bumpers met with a gentle tap.

I backed away on my own side of the road and called over an apology. A cheery English voice called back, "That's all right, Yank."

We dropped off the VW outside London because I wasn't quite ready to try city driving, stayed one more night at the Chelsea Arts

Club and enjoyed a fine flight back to New York. I was happy to have seen London at peace and with children back on the streets and in the parks.

Our time in London was so enjoyable in so many ways that I felt I had experienced all the rewards and pleasures that the social side of book publishing had to offer.

As soon as I got back to work at McKay I found a major difference between working for an established, well-known imprint, and a firm well liked by its authors, but not widely known within the industry. The Rawsons had published several large scale bestsellers including *Everything You Always Wanted To Know About Sex But Were Afraid To Ask,* and *The Hidden Persuaders* by Vance Packard. They were reputable, helpful and enormously saleable books, but the editorial framework that had produced these books was in the good hands of Ken and Eleanor Rawson. They looked to me for books that represented different interests in different fields.

At the big-name firms where I had worked in the past the literary agents frequently sent us the best of the work of the authors they represented. This was not true at McKay, so I began to exert all the friendly pressure I could on the ranking agents to let us have first look at some of the properties they were most excited about. It was very pleasurable work. I made regular luncheon and cocktail dates with Helen Strauss of the William Morris Agency, Phyllis Jackson and Kay Brown from MCA, Willis Wing, Carol and Carl Brandt, Don Congdon, Belle Rosenbaum and Pat Duggan—before he went to work for Sam Goldwyn.

The first book I worked with over a period of several months was a new biography of Will Rogers by Donald Day. Donald was a rangy, exuberant writer, teacher and former editor of the prestigious Southwest Review. His interest in Will Rogers was a lifelong commitment and his book reflected this. Donald's only weakness as a writer was his inability to cool the intensity of his enthusiasms which led him to use sentences and paragraphs overloaded with colorful adjectives and adverbs. More than once I had to remind him of an art teacher I had heard of who said that it took two people to create a good painting—one to put on the paint and the other to tell him when to stop.

Will Rogers had been a hero and delight to me ever since I heard his first radio broadcast and read his column. Donald's marvelously detailed biography was a joy to work on. There are many people who claim that he was the greatest native American humorist who ever lived.

Will's grandmother was a Cherokee Indian and his parents both had Indian blood. Will used to say he didn't know enough mathematics to figure out what percentage Cherokee he was. But as a boy he had heard the heartbreaking story of The Trail of Tears from his grandmother who had survived the brutal forced march of 17,000 Cherokees from their native lands in Georgia to lands in the far West. The Cherokee Nation was a civilized, literate tribe with its own constitution based on the U.S. model. They were a peaceful, industrious people who lived in the beautiful, fertile valley of the Tennessee River, and over a period of years they had ceded huge areas of their homeland to accommodate the move westward of the white settlers.

Beginning in 1830 the Georgia legislature began to pass laws disenfranchising the Cherokee Nation. Indians were deprived of all legal rights and driven like animals to lands in the west that nobody wanted.

Rogers pointed out frequently that the politicians in Washington had signed many treaties with Indians in various parts of the country, all of which ended with the covenant that the treaty would be observed "as long as the grass grows and the waters run." Not one of these treaties was ever kept. Rogers observed that the matter had been finally solved by moving the Indians to land where there was neither grass nor water.

His humor was always pointed, but it was never vicious. His targets were politicians and political bodies that put private reward before public good. One of his remarks that I read first in Donald's book concerned our method for electing the nation's president.

"The high office of the U.S. has degenerated into two ordinarily fine men, being goaded on by their political leeches, into saying things that if they were in their right minds they wouldn't dream of saying... Now instead of calling each other names till next Tuesday, why you can do everybody a big favor by going fishing...then come back next Wednesday and we will let you know which one is the lesser of two evils."

With no evidence at all, I have a hunch that Will Rogers had warmer feelings for Calvin Coolidge than any American president except FDR. On his way to meet Coolidge for the first time Will bet that he could make Coolidge smile. The bet was taken. Will was formally introduced, and as the President put out his hand Will said, "Sorry, I didn't catch the name."

The two men had several meetings. Will reported that at one visit he had started off by asking the President what sort of crooks and horse thiefs he had met that day.

The President looked at him, Rogers wrote, with that weaned-on-a-pickle look, and replied: "the cabinet." Clearly the two men had something in common.

Soon after Rogers death in a plane crash in Alaska, Carl Sandburg wrote: "There is a curious parallel between Will Rogers and Abraham Lincoln. They were rare figures whom we could call beloved with ease and without embarrassment."

One of the major book clubs took Donald's book and it sold well. Frequently, when I have had a hand in the publishing of biographies, I remember the words of an Egyptian scribe who, four thousand years before the coming of printing from moveable type, wrote: "A man has perished and his body has become earth. It is writing that makes him remembered." Would anyone, I wondered, remember the name of the great Theban ruler Ozymandias were it not for Shelley's bitter, ironic poem?

As all publishers know, some books just happen to come your way but others you have to go out and get. Back in my days at Harcourt we had published several stunningly good sports books for "younger" readers by John Tunis. The involvement of Americans of all ages with sport was booming and I set out on a search for an author to write a group of novels recreating the careers of young men and women in the major sports fields.

By some miraculous piece of luck I ran across Tex Maule who was a working sports writer, an ex tight-end for the San Francisco 49'ers and a student of creative writing. Tex did some fine books for McKay and he and I became friends. One line he wrote in an article for Sports Illustrated gives me great pleasure every time I think of it. Tex was writing a summer survey of the National Football League's fall season. He took up the teams one by one and estimated their strengths and weaknesses. At that time The Washington Redskins team was owned by George Marshall who was most reluctant to sign contracts with black players no matter how good they were. He had a very promising, very young, very white quarterback named Norm Snead. When Tex got around to rating the chances of the Redskins he wrote: "Norm Snead faces the lightest huddle and the darkest future of any quarterback in the NFL."

Editing is hardly a precise profession. Many times, if you are an experienced literary doctor, you can help the author find a cure for an ailing manuscript. And lots of times you can't, or the treatment you recommend doesn't appeal to the author. One fine novel we published at McKay was *Anna Teller* by Jo Sinclair whose first novel had won the Harper Prize. I never did learn how it came to Eleanor Rawson at McKay, but soon after I joined the firm Eleanor suggested that I become Jo's editor. I read the manuscript and was impressed and excited. The book was the story of a Hungarian grandmother who had fought Russian tanks in the streets of Budapest, escaped to the United States and was making a new life for herself and her family. Anna was a remarkable woman who came vividly to life in the pages of the manuscript—so did a pair of married relatives. The problem, it seemed to me, was that the troubles of the young couple were so vividly drawn that they gradually took the focus away from Anna. I wrote Jo several letters in the attempt to explain the difficulty I felt that readers would have with the changing nature of the book's dramatic structure. Correspondence on my reservations didn't accomplish anything and Jo invited me to come out and spend a few days with her in Ohio to talk it over.

I had a good visit with her, but she didn't like my solution to a problem that she didn't believe existed. I tried to make her see that the young couple's adjustment to life in the United States really deserved a book of their own instead of running competition to a reader's commitment to the irresistibly compelling figure of Anna. Jo had the final word of course. It wasn't a question of winning or losing, it was simply a difference of opinion between two people with the same goal but with differing feelings about how to reach it.

When the book was published many reviewers stated their reservations about precisely the same dimension that Jo and I had disagreed about. We sold the United Kingdom rights to a London publisher whose editor took the same position that I had. This time Jo agreed, so the British edition appeared without the young couple. It was a successful book in both countries. The London reviews were positive without reservations, but Jo wrote me later that she really liked the American edition better.

A working editor comes by books to publish in many different ways. Some manuscripts come over the transom when the office is closed. Others come by mail, delivered by hand to your office or home, handed to you on a train or in a restaurant. No matter how they reach you they deserve attention. Most editors believe that nothing matters as much as the creative spirit of men and women and you start reading every manuscript with the hope that it will turn out to be a book you can publish with excitement and confidence.

One morning at McKay I got a telephone call from a man I had grown up with in St. Albans, Vermont. I hadn't heard from him in more than twenty years and I didn't remember him all that well. It turned out that he, Bob Brush, was an executive assistant to Mr. Ernest Henderson who was president and CEO of the Sheraton Hotel chain. Mr. Henderson had written the story of his life and Bob wanted to know if I would be willing to read it. He went on to say that Mr. Henderson had an offer from Doubleday, but there was something about the offer that Mr. Henderson didn't like.

I told Bob that I'd be glad to read it. The manuscript arrived by messenger. I took it home and read it over the weekend, liked it and called Bob on Monday. I asked what Doubleday's position in the matter was. Bob said that Doubleday liked it well enough to make a publication contract, but Mr. Henderson had hinted that he would like to buy a substantial number of copies (to put in thousands of hotel rooms?) and Doubleday wanted the quantity specified in the contract.

Mr. Henderson was going to buy a lot of copies, Bob told me, but he really wanted a publisher who thought it was good enough to be published without this kind of guaranteed sale. I told Bob that

I wouldn't make any kind of offer until I had a chance to discuss editorial matters with the author. Bob asked me if I really liked the book and I told him I liked the book as it was, but it could be improved with judicious cutting, elimination of flashbacks and a certain amount of re-writing.

The following week I had a meeting with Mr. Henderson. He was a low-keyed, soft-spoken and gracious man with whom I felt at ease very quickly. Bob had told him I wanted some changes in the text and he asked me to explain what they were and why I felt they were needed. He listened closely, asked a few more questions and then said:

"If I make the changes you want will your firm publish the book?" I said my firm would be delighted to publish the book.

Mr. Henderson gave me a quizzical glance. "What about the copies that Bob told you I might want to buy?"

"We can talk about that when the time comes," I said, "the first thing we have to do is make sure this manuscript gets to be as good as we can make it."

We finished the book without major arguments. One of the most difficult problems editors have with inexperienced writers is to get them to believe that if they say something well enough once they don't have to say it again for emphasis or clarity. Ernest Henderson was a quick study and he had a fine, interesting purely American story to tell.

After graduating from Harvard, Ernest Henderson formed what was to be a lifetime partnership with his classmate Robert Moore. One of their first business ventures was the ownership of a modest store that, among other things, sold menswear. Mr. Henderson's telling of an incident in this venture, one of my favorite anecdotes in the whole, lively book, concerns their purchase, at a spectacularly low price, of a large number of mens' suits from a European manufacturer. The styling was correct, the workmanship reasonably good and the retail price—allowing for a healthy mark-up— was irresistible. Everything was going well until one of their first customers was caught in the rain wearing one of the suits. His suit dissolved and he was very unhappy to say the least.

The partners' reaction to this gloomy event was to refund the customer's money and seek out every purchaser of one of these particular suits. This kind of responsible, simple honesty which was to mark all their future business dealings left them with a lot of suits that they had paid for, and in all propriety could sell only to men who would never wear them in the rain.

After some concentrated thinking they came up with the solution. They offered the suits at a most attractive price in a mail order campaign directed to New England undertakers. The suits sold out very quickly and there were no dissatisfied customers.

As Ernest Henderson and Robert Moore began to develop the Sheraton Hotel chain they formulated ten business commandments for themselves and for all Sheraton executives. The tenth commandment was "Thou shalt not take the last penny out of any business transaction." The other commandments all reflected the same kind of thinking. The book was published with the title *The World of Mr. Sheraton,* received complimentary reviews, and sold a respectable number of copies both in hardbound and paper editions in addition to the large bulk order from Mr. Henderson. Altogether a very pleasant publishing experience. I did sense a difference between Ernest Henderson and Conrad Hilton. Mr. Hilton was more visibly the image of the entrepreneur who saw his success in terms of profit. Ernest Henderson seemed no less concerned with profit, but his real reward was the pleasure he took in being a popular and successful innkeeper.

McKay had a very successful children's book department, and after a trip to a paper mill I wrote a story about how a little spruce tree became a book that a child could hold in his hand. Its title was *From This to That.* Our children's book editor liked it enough to publish it, the Junior Literary Guild chose it for distribution and I had a book club selection to celebrate.

However, in less than two years I began to feel restless and uneasy. I've never been able to identify all the factors that contributed to my cheerless frame of mind, but the climate of book publishing seemed to be changing. Hardly a month went by without the announcement of a new merger or takeover. One by one independent publishers became new profit centers for conglomerates.

At McKay I was working with colleagues that I admired and trusted. Quent Bossi was the finest of men and sales managers. My old friend, Ted Mills, was a valued and perceptive ally. In the advertising and promotion area Carolyn Anthony did a splendid, creative

job. My relationship with the Rawsons was pleasant but imper-
sonal and there was certainly nothing in my immediate publishing
situation to make me uncomfortable. It was, however, the first time
in my publishing life that I had no part in the stimulating areas of
sales, promotion and advertising. I was not a publisher, I was an editor and the demands of that job were changing too.

Growing up as a book lover, I believed that writing splendid
books made people famous. The change that I felt coming was that
in the future books would be written by, for, or about people who
were already famous. I agreed with the dismal pronouncement of
Andy Warhol, that famous painter of canned soup, that in years to
come everybody would be famous for fifteen minutes. This would
be a tough market place for a book editor.

New York was changing too. There was pollution in the atmos-
phere, danger on the streets, violence in formerly pleasant neighborhoods and you couldn't walk in Central Park after dark. I spent
about four hours a day traveling by car and train from my home to
my office and back again. More and more my mind kept going to
a book I wanted very much to write.

In 1956 I had visited Carl Sandburg at his home in North
Carolina. Ever since the days we had worked on the Lincoln biography together I had urged Carl to write a book on Lincoln's
humor, how he used it and how it had saved his sanity during the
most fearful years of the American presidency. The night before I
left to return to New York I had brought up the matter again. Carl
spoke of how much he liked the books I had done on the humor
of New England and said he really didn't want to do the Lincoln
book I had urged him to do. "You do it," he said. I agreed to do my
best and we shook hands for the last time.

Now it was clearly time to remember the advice that my friends
and I had so often laid on young people who wanted to become
writers: "No matter how much you want to write be sure to keep
one foot on somebody's payroll."

The only paying job I could think of that would give me both the
time and freedom to research and write the Lincoln book was as a
New England sales representative of a Boston or New York publisher. This would take me back to the bookstores, which I'd enjoy,
and keep me traveling in a part of the country that I knew and
loved. Emily and I could rent the house we had bought not far from

the one that had burned down, and live in the family Vermont homestead which my mother had been maintaining, alone, since my father died.

There was much backing and forthing on this decision, but we finally decided to take the gamble after Viking said I would be most welcome to sell any New England territory I wanted to.

The family Vermont homestead had been named Rockledge by my father. In the 1920's, when he and other people were making impressive sums of money in the stock market, north and south wings were added to the beautiful old farmhouse. That was when he discovered the house was built on a ledge of some of the most stubborn rock in northern Vermont.

When Emily and I moved in we chose the large north bedroom which I had occupied with my older brother. We changed the old beds for our newer ones but left the rest of the room the way it had always been. The Maxfield Parrish print had gone with my sister, but all the books were still there. I spent one afternoon sitting on the window seat re- reading some of them. I may have worried that this time their magic would be gone, but found it was just as potent as it had been so long ago.

Little John knocked Robin off the log bridge; Myles Falworth once more slew the wicked Duke of Alban to clear his father's name; young Idas lay wounded with beauty in the summer night; each man killed the thing he loved in a prison that I (to myself) pro-nounced like the name of a high wind; the smiling boy who brought the good news fell dead; distant young voices from the playing fields of Eton still cried "play up, play up and play the game," and Tom Swift spoke as adverbially as ever.

It was wonderful to be out of the city and back in Vermont. My salesman's itinerary took me into five of the New England states three times a year. I was never away from home for more than a week at a time and there were highly productive months between trips. It felt great calling on booksellers again. Many of them I had met at the American Booksellers Annual convention, so many friendships were renewed and new friends made.

The humorous Lincoln project went well. I had bought the big set of all the writings of Abraham Lincoln and the best of the volumes of contemporary sources: his law partner Herndon and his White House assistants Nicolay and Hay, as well as Ida Tarbell's fine biography. One aspect of research disturbed me. Many of Mr. Lincoln's remarks were quoted by people who heard them first hand at the same time but reported them differently. I finally decided to use the versions I liked best.

Whenever I was away from the writing project my mind kept returning to publishing.

Victor Weybright, a brilliant, controversial publisher had written in his autobiography, "I believe that, as a publisher, I am personally responsible for prompt attention to the welfare of my authors, of the book trade and of the readers."

The reference to the welfare of the readers interested me. To my mind it was the reason we put so much emphasis on the quality of the design and materials that constituted the finished book. The binding, the paper, and the type face were all parts of the aesthetics of the book reading experience. One pleasant custom that book publishers once observed was to present the authors of new books with handsome leather-bound copies of the first edition of their books at Christmastime of the year in which they were published.

During WW II book production codes led to pages crammed with small type, and bound with materials that were substitutes for the tough buckram, cotton and traditional linen fabrics. But, as cost accountants were quick to point out, book sales were booming so maybe good design and first quality components didn't matter that much after all.

Many hours, while driving, I ran a sort of retrospective mental film of all the changes that I had seen in my cherished industry.

I saw myself poking around in depot wastebaskets in Italy and France in the 1930's looking for Tauchnitz editions of books in English. These were the first paperbound editions I had seen and I loved them. Apparently many people bought books to read on trains and when they got to the end of their trip they threw them away the way Americans got rid of magazines. Oddly enough,

Americans never did seem to get used to throwing paperback books away.

The paperback revolution in the U.S. was an astonishing literary explosion. It made it possible for a person of the most modest means to own a library that would have been the envy of the very wealthy in times past. Not too long after WW II it appeared that almost every publisher was putting out a paperback line of books. Marketing moguls found paperback book outlets in thousands of stores that had never offered books of any kind before. All these hundreds of titles were put on the market on a fully returnable basis. The distributor could send back all unsold copies.

During one period a paperback publisher could do nothing with his mountain of unsold books except, as I heard it, ship them to Western New York State where they were needed as landfill for a construction project.

A black humor report had it that a certain paperback publisher had become so depressed at the number of books that had been returned for credit that he tried to commit suicide by jumping out of the window of his office on the 20th story of a skyscraper. The attempt failed however; the thousands and thousands of returned books had been stacked against the side of the building and he only fell twenty feet.

Wherever I went around New England and whoever I was with, the conversation always revolved around books and publishing. Frequently there discussions of the always changing publishing scene—who bought whom for how much and who had lost jobs as a result. I was kept pretty much up to date on what was going on in New York and Boston even though I rarely got to either scene of publishing action. When I thought about the years I had spent in publishing I concluded I had traveled all the roads there were on the publishing map, made all the stops and enjoyed reaching all interim destinations. When I looked into the future I saw no return to publishing. But naturally things changed and I'm not quite sure what it was that outlined a new challenge for me.

Perhaps it all started one night when my mother, Emily and I were sitting around the fireplace after dinner with several of my mother's friends. The talk, of course, turned to books and reading. At first the talk was general, then the conversation seemed to center around the problem my mother and her friends were having reading new books and old favorites because the type was too small. Magnifying devices decreased reading pleasure to a sorry degree.

"Why," a guest asked, "doesn't somebody put out books in a type size that we can read easily?"

I said I didn't know and we began to talk, carefully, about matters relating to the minister and some of the members of the congregation of our little church.

When I woke up the next morning the type-size dilemma hit me with much more impact than it had the night before. Why indeed? Here were six well-educated people in their sixties or early seventies whose lifelong reading pleasure was being diminished or denied by a minor design detail. How many people were there in our society who had the same complaint, and how could the publishing industry's responsibility to them be fulfilled?

I couldn't stop thinking about the unique experience of reading a book, how much it had meant to me and to millions of others of all ages. To close the world of reading to anyone, of any age, for so insignificant a reason as the size of the type was cruel, unusual and clearly not to be tolerated by an industry with any sense of its social accountability.

Some time in the past, perhaps motivated by the popular laws of an unidentifiable Murphy, I had concocted a law of my own. I called it Jennison's law of instantaneous gradualism —We will do everything slowly and carefully but we'll do it right now. I wrote the Library of Congress Division of the Blind and Physically Handicapped and asked some questions. Until the moment I typed the letter it had not occurred to me that there might be many people with perfect eyesight who could not enjoy the book reading experience due to another kind of disability. The tone of the reply, which came quickly, suggested that there was a real need for large type, or large print, books by six or eight million people. We editors, especially those who were selecting titles for conglomerate profit centers, were always being chided for not doing enough market research. The thought came urgently to my mind that a publisher of books in large type would have a superb source, not only of detailed information on the market, but also on how to serve the market. I answered the first letter by asking a lot more questions. This time the reply came even more promptly and concluded by suggesting that I come down to Washington to discuss the matter. The visit introduced me to Robert Bray, one of the finest men and most devoted public servants who ever fought for the rights of handicapped Americans. I worked closely with him for several years and am convinced that without him and his dedicated colleagues and staff the large-type publishing program might never have gotten started.

When I got back from Washington I began to widen my market research by writing all the organizations I could find who were committed to services to the blind and handicapped. The answers came quickly and enthusiastically. All of them had the same major theme: there was a great need for large-type reading materials and nobody seemed to be doing much about it.

As the months passed I became more and more certain that there was a reachable market to support a specialized publishing operation. Clearly the next step was to find out exactly what size type would serve the most common form of visual impairment. There wasn't much medical research on this but there was enough, with the help of Dr. Jack Prince of the Institute for Research and Vision at Ohio State University, to come to the conclusion that 18-point type would probably serve more visually impaired persons than any other size.

It had been obvious from the beginning that if (and at that point it was still if) I did set out to publish books for these readers I would not be able to order new composition for the books—it would be too expensive. I would have to make photo enlargements of the pages of books already in print which would mean larger books. Other characters of the books would be demanding. The paper must be off-white to cut down glare, of very high opacity to prevent distracting show-through, and very supple so that a page once turned would stay turned—flat and readable. Only the best binding materials would be appropriate for what would surely be years of multiple readings. Some preliminary experiments indicated that the books should measure 8-1/2 x 11 inches to conform to the requirements of standard printing and binding equipment. Finding the right paper was tedious. I found out that to get exactly the paper I wanted I would have to have it specially made. One of the smaller mills accepted the challenge and finally created a beautiful, acid-free sheet, that wouldn't turn yellow or brittle for a hundred years.

Over the months, detail by detail, the publishing project took shape. In the fall of 1963 the Lincoln book was finished and I sent it off to my agent in New York to see if he could find a publisher for it. I had many melancholy hours and days re-reading material on the assassination of Abraham Lincoln while trying to raise my spirit from the depression that followed the assassination of John Kennedy.

There was my own personal sorrow. On a sunny morning in June 1963 while my mother and I were having morning coffee she complained of a terrible headache, put out her hand for me to hold and died. I shall always be grateful I was with her.

In the spring I had the publishing program well planned and ready to present to possible sources of capitalization. I had cost figures, sales projections, growth patterns based on data I had learned from experience with publishing programs.

Viking was the first firm I approached for many reasons. In the first place I had thought up this project while I was on their payroll and the old-fashioned precept was that when an employee conceived a new product he offered it first to the firm he was working for. Viking's response was encouraging and they agreed to consider the proposal.

It was evident that all the preliminary work that could be done on the large-type program outside New York had been completed. We notified our tenant in the Rockland County house that we'd like to move back in as soon as possible and were happy to hear that she was about to notify us that she would like to move out. This fortuitous response was matched by a request, from a woman we knew and liked, to rent Rockledge for an indeterminate period thus clearing the way for our return to the New York area.

There was, of course, an immediate need for capital. We had enough money to maintain ourselves for a limited period and a small bit of working capital to put into the new business, but beyond that the future looked chancy.

The Hotel Shelton at Lexington and 49th Street had one floor devoted to small offices that could be rented and furnished by the month, complete with telephone service and secretarial service if necessary. I rented one and went to work.

My time was divided between making sample pages of books to show prospective investors what the product would look like and making dates with publishers and individuals who might want to back the project. After lengthy consideration Viking decided not to take part in the program.

There were a series of very heartening interviews with publishers and interested book people. They agreed that there probably was a great need for books like mine, but did not think a publishing program limited to this one kind of book would be profitable enough to stay alive. Then there were the disheartening discussions which ended with the judgement that if this was a good publishing idea it would have been done long ago.

Bob Bray and his people at the Library of Congress were very supportive and frequently put me in touch with men and women who might help get the program started. The months went by.

The more intimately acquainted I became with the potential readership the more fervently I believed in the program. In one meeting it was pointed out to me that there were millions of people who had no source of printed news that they could read.

The thought came that the *News of the Week in Review* section of the Sunday *New York Times* reprinted in 18 point type would be a real boon to many, many people. I did some enlarging and pasting up of a sample issue and, through friends, made an appointment to present the idea to Ivan Veit—one of the *Times* Vice-Presidents.

Mr. Veit accepted the sample material and market projections and said that he thought the idea might have merit and I would be hearing from them.

Several weeks later I was invited to a meeting at the *Times* office. Mr. Veit presided and led a friendly informal discussion of the whole concept of reading materials for the handicapped. Mr. Veit finally said that the *Times* had decided that they did want to put out a large type edition. He looked at me inquiringly:

"What we can't figure out, Mr. Jennison, is what there is in this for you."

I answered that the appearance of such a publication would be a great help to my program. The problem, as I saw it, was that existing materials and devices had overtones of therapy instead of pleasure. I said that I was going to publish a lot of books in large type and that I needed a new climate in which they could be accepted and enjoyed without the suggestion of remedial materials for the handicapped.

"There's a line of Sandburg's that answers your question Mr. Veit. 'One hand washes the other but both wash the face.' You're going to give me a fine place to advertise my books."

At one meeting in Chicago I met a woman who had a visually impaired daughter. She was deeply interested in my program and asked if I would meet her on her next trip to New York.

When she called I suggested she come to my office and see the sample materials, list of books I planned to publish and operation budgets. She seemed more interested than ever and asked me for a round figure of how much money I thought I'd need to get the program under way. The figure I gave her didn't seem to discourage her at all.

About two weeks later she called from the Cosmopolitan Club and asked me if I could have lunch with her. Soon after we sat down she told me that she could arrange the financing for me.

I've forgotten what we had for lunch.

When I got back to the Shelton Hotel I went into the bar to have a celebratory drink and ran into my old friend Franklin Watts. Frank was a book salesman/publisher whom I had known and liked for years. He asked me what I was up to and I said why didn't he come upstairs and I'd show him.

He went over all the material with what seemed to be growing interest. Then he asked me how soon I was going to get some books on the market.

"As soon as I can," I said, "I just got the capital committed about an hour ago."

"Do you really want to start a new firm?"

His question raised a basic consideration that I had been dodging for months. I wondered if he sensed that what I really wanted was a business I wanted to work in but didn't want to run.

I asked him what the alternative was.

Frank told me the story of his own entry into publishing and how after he had become successful had sold his firm to Grolier so he wouldn't have to worry about financing and re- financing, but would be left alone to publish the books he wanted to publish the way he wanted to publish them.

"They're fine people," Frank said, "and great to work with."

All I knew about Grolier was that they published *The Book of Knowledge* and various encyclopedias.

"Come up and talk to the president with me," Frank said, "you could move in with me, use any of my people you wanted to and hire your own as you need them."

It was tempting but I needed time to think it over. Frank said he understood and would be glad to hear from me as soon as I wanted to go into more details.

The more I thought about it the more I liked it. Frank and I were old friends and traveling companions. We wouldn't have to spend much time getting to know each other. So a week later I met with Frank and Ed McCabe, president of Grolier, and I presented the case for large-type books. Mr. McCabe went over my rough projections of costs and sales, asked a few pertinent questions and agreed to add my operation to the already successful Franklin Watts Division. I never regretted the affiliation for a moment. The Chicago lady accepted this solution enthusiastically.

Soon I had a desk and an invaluable assistant in the person of an attractive young lady whose Scottish accent was delightful. Anne

Scoullar had a fine, quick mind, incomparable secretarial skills and the conviction that the only way to do a job was to do it right.

While Anne took care of the office I went hunting for editions of the books I wanted to reprint. The search took me into the stores of rare-book dealers in search of limited editions, to miles of aisles in second-hand book stores, to the card files of the New York Public Library to check on different editions of the same book. Once in a while I would buy a multi-volume set of a classic author because I knew that I would want to publish several of the titles in my series.

One of the most welcome finds was a limited edition set of the works of Charles Dickens printed (to the delight of Anne S.) in Edinburg in 1907. The bindings were faded but the paper and printing were superb. Another treasure was discovered in a small shop on Fourth Avenue. This was a limited edition of the works of Jane Austen beautifully produced by an American printer with charming illustrations.

Perhaps the volume that pleased and excited me most was a limited edition of Edith Wharton's great short novel, *Ethan Frome*. Charles Scribner's Sons had commissioned Bruce Rogers—possibly the most celebrated American designer and printer—to produce a special edition of the distinguished work. The result was a masterpiece of bookmaking.

Frank had made up his mind that the imprint for the new books should be Keith Jennison Books. It wouldn't have been my first choice, but it was a custom that had some currency in book publishing and I couldn't think of anything I liked better. So we began. I sent out news releases to the major book media describing the program and the need for it. As several prospective investors had commented, there was no way the idea of publishing in large type could be protected anymore than the concept of selling pre-sliced loaves of bread could be trademarked. I felt, along with a general whose name I have forgotten, that in a campaign like this you tried to make sure you got there firstest with the mostest men, so I announced that I had a list of four hundred titles that I was going to put into print as quickly as possible. In fact I had a longer list than that, made up from sources I had used constantly during twenty-five years in the world of books. I had also studied the fine Wilson Catalogues for Public Libraries, High School libraries and Junior High School libraries with special attention to the ratings accorded to the Wilson consultants. I was looking for books that, over the years, had proved to have an ever-renewing readership. The early lists contained books by John Steinbeck, Zane Gray, Dorothy L. Sayers, Rachel Carson, Mark Twain, R.L. Stevenson, Edith Wharton, William Shakespeare and other great names in literary history.

Seeking the right binding process took much research. I had to have books that lay flat when opened and whose bindings performed their function through countless readings. All the manufacturing specifications were finally met and I had the thrill of going to the printers and watching the books being printed and bound.

The first title to come off the press was *Profiles in Courage* by John Kennedy—a selection one reviewer called "appropriate." One by one, reprint contracts were signed with the original publishers of the books I wanted and I started a year of traveling that was rewarding beyond my expectations. I called on the major libraries and school systems from Augusta, Maine to Seattle, Washington.

Before I made my first call I had worried that librarians and teachers would say, "Large type, what for?" Instead I heard, over and over again, 'Where have you been, we've been waiting for you for twenty-five years."

One of the most exciting areas was concerned with large-type text books for the visually handicapped in the school systems. Over and over I was asked for enlarged editions of textbooks that had been adopted for state-wide use so a few visually or physically impaired students could stay in their regular classes. The books were made—some of them huge in size and price but, as several teachers told me, invaluable to the students who needed them. We could even make one large-type copy of a book for a particular student who needed it.

During one visit to Washington for a meeting with Bob Bray and his colleagues at the Library of Congress I had the good fortune to meet Harold Russell, chairman of the President's Council on Employment of the Handicapped. Harold, a seaman whose forearms had been blown off in a WW II naval battle, had won an *Oscar* for his only acting appearance in *The Best Years of Our Lives*—a 1946 war movie that had been hailed as a masterpiece.

Harold pointed out that my program was directly related to his and asked me to become a member of the Council.

As the months passed the response to the books widened and deepened. We got many reports from libraries about the wonderful reactions of people who discovered the books for the first time. Some libraries reported that they were seeing readers they hadn't seen for years because they were shy about bringing enlarging devices when they came to the library to read. The 18-point books they could read with ease. Younger library patrons were taking large-type books home for elderly parents or friends with Parkinson's or MS.

Of all the days that remain fresh in my memory there was one particular day that seems to contain the essence of the whole experience. Harold Russell, Bob Bray and I spent the day on Long Island visiting a library and a rehab hospital.

In the library we saw, prominently shelved, all my large type titles. At one table an older man was looking up something in our recently published large-type edition of the Columbia-Viking Desk Encyclopedia. Apparently he had just been using the Hammond-Jennison *Large Type World Atlas* as well. The librarian, with considerable excitement, told us that he had just heard of a new use for the large type books. They turned out to be great for speed reading.

At the rehab hospital we stood beside the incredibly complex wheel chair of a frail teen-age girl who had limited head and arm movement. An adjustable tray with a book on it was set at the right level for reading. The tray held a book to which was attached an automatic page turner.

"Let's try one of your books," Harold said.

A nurse took away the automated page turner and put down one of my oversize editions.

Slowly the girl reached out a pencil-thin arm, flipped open the cover and slipped a finger beneath one of the pages. The page curled over and lay flat. The words were clear and black against the ivory paper. She looked up with a smile that melted us.

"I...can...do...it...myself."

In another ward we stopped beside an amazing sling-like contraption that raised and lowered the body of a young boy lying face down with his head supported by a canvas strap over a round hole in the sling.

"Automobile accident." The attendant said. The sling had been lowered so the boy's face was about a foot above the floor. I saw his head move and realized he was turning the pages of a book with a rubber-tipped wand he held in his mouth. The book was one of mine. The name of the character told me which one.

The boy had lost almost everything but at least, for a while, free from the sterile, white, hospital prison, he was with Jim Hawkins, Squire Trelawney and Long John Silver aboard the Hispaniola sailing the blue waters of the Spanish Main.

The press had greeted my large-type publishing program warmly and enthusiastically with comments such as, "Our only wonder is that someone didn't think years ago of this gift to the tired, the ill, the aging and the millions deprived for various reasons of this ease and comfort in reading."

In our first business year we did about $50,000. In the second year $500,000 and in our third almost $1,000,000. The management of Watts and Grolier was delighted. Of course we didn't dominate the field for very long. Putting books in large-type was not a patentable process and soon several publishers began to issue some of their titles in large-type formats instead of licensing the editions to us. But that was good for the cause. The potential appeal of large-type editions was far too large to be satisfied by a single publisher. Now the concept was a working reality and my work was done.

Book publishing in general was becoming big business in every sense of the word. Huge international corporations were acquiring small publishers by the dozen. All these conglomerates were totally dedicated not to the improvement of the product, but to the maximization of profit.

As a vice-president in a division of Franklin Watts, which was a division of Grolier, which was in turn part of a larger publishing empire, I felt uneasy and unqualified for more years of book publishing. I wanted to get back to writing and I wanted to get back to Vermont.

After much thought and planning we moved to a beautiful small college town in central Vermont. We revived some old friendships and made many new ones. The college gave me the opportunity to teach a generation of young men and women some of the fundamentals of professional writing and publishing and to become part of their lives.

POST SCRIPT

Now, those years seem both very close and very far away. This account doesn't prove anything except that you have to live in your own time and if you are lucky, as I was, it will be a good one.

I wrote this book mostly in Vermont in a pleasant room surrounded by books and photographs of many of the men and women who made my time so rewarding. Most of them have died by now, but they have not passed away. They are just as much with me as they were when they wrote greetings on their likenesses—and just as alive as the great musicians and composers whose music I listen to with increasing appreciation.

Two citations honoring the large-type program hang on the wall of my work room. The first is a Carey-Thomas Honorable Mention Award for Creative Publishing in 1966, and the second the award of the Joseph Campbell medal from the American Library Association for service to the blind.

At the time I left New York to come home to Vermont there were two publishers of large print/type books at an annual rate of about 120 titles. In 1989 eight major publishers were producing more than 1200 titles per year. The use of large-type materials in all categories has exceeded my most optimistic projections and is growing rapidly.

I think my feeling about my part in this development has something to do with what Francis Bacon wrote, so long ago:

"I hold every man a debtor to his profession...."

KWJ